HAL•LEONARD®

GUITAR PLAY-ALONG

AUDIO ACCESS INCLUDED

Minor BLUES

T0039675

CONTENTS

PLAYBACK+
Speed • Pitch • Balance • Loop

To access audio visit:
www.halleonard.com/mylibrary

Enter Code
6114-2625-4374-0153

ISBN 978-1-4950-4591-2

HAL•LEONARD®
7777 W. BLUEMOUND RD. P.O. BOX 13819 MILWAUKEE, WI 53213

Visit Hal Leonard Online at
www.halleonard.com

As the Years Go Passing By

Words and Music by Deadric Malone

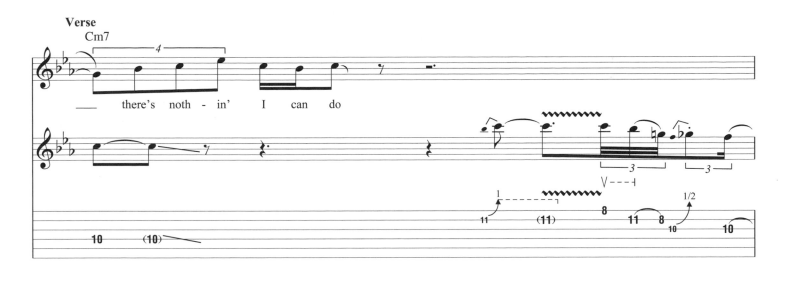

Verse

Cm7

there's noth-in' I can do

Fm7   Cm7

if you leave   me here to cry.

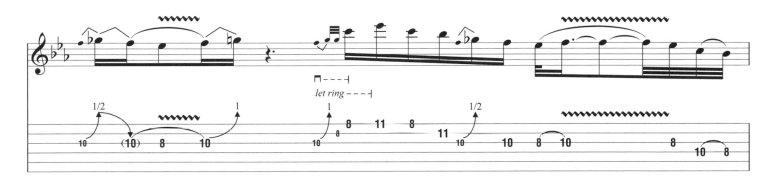

Fm7

_Yeah, __ there's   noth-in' I   can   do ___

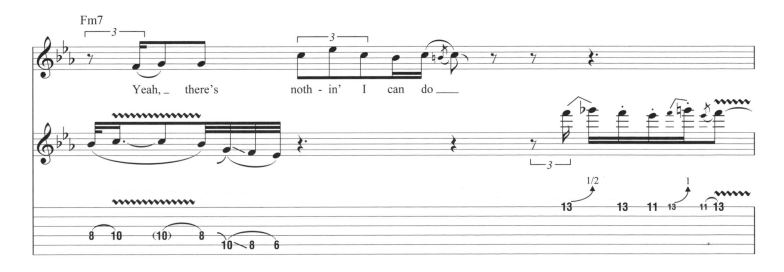

if you leave   me here to   cry. ____

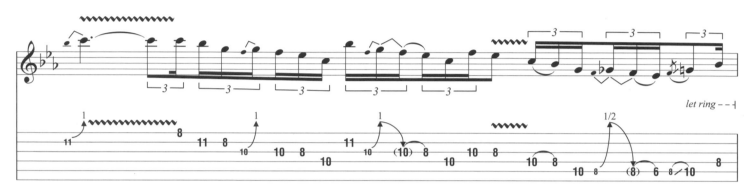

let ring – – ┤

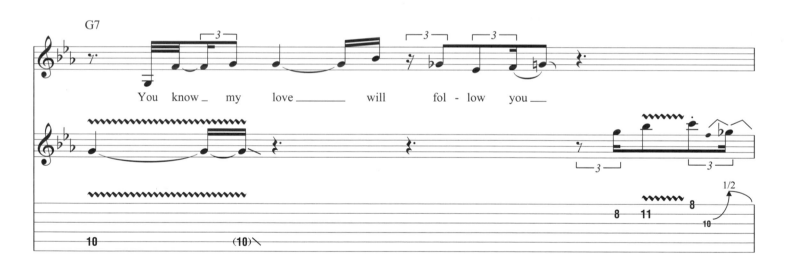

You know__ my   love _____   will   fol - low   you __

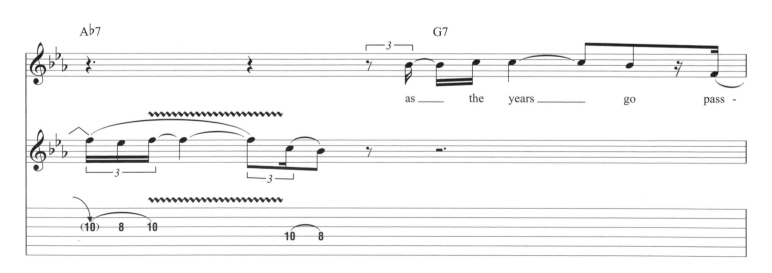

as ____   the   years _____   go   pass -

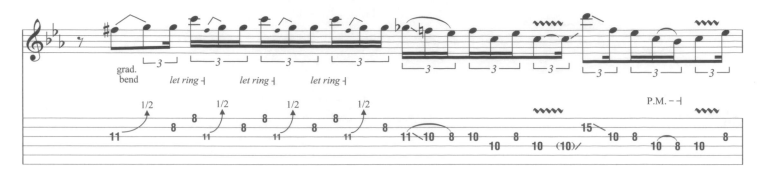

Fm7

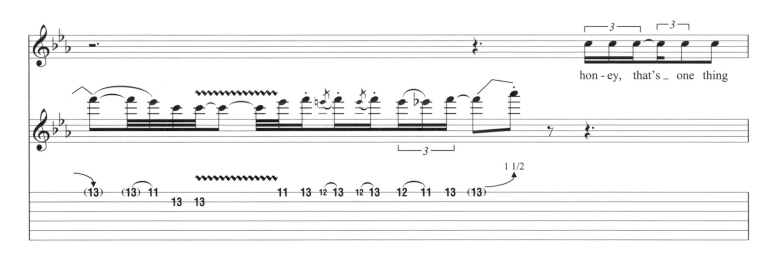

I gave _____ you all _____ I owned, _

honey, that's _ one thing

Cm7

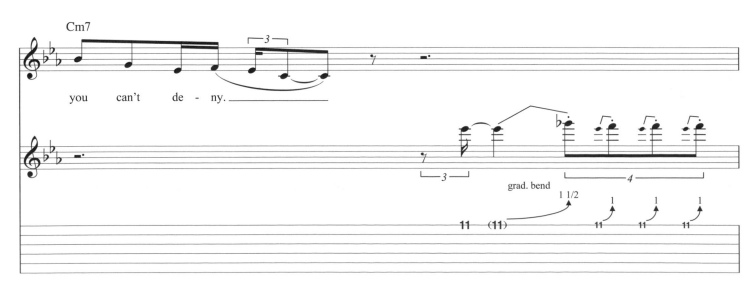

you can't de-ny. _____

6

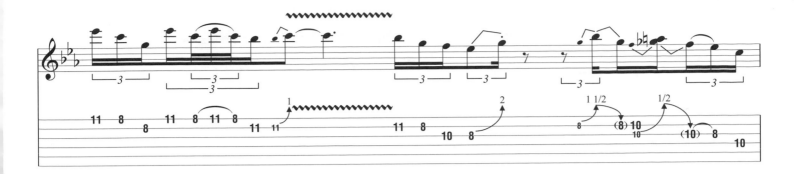

Know my love __ will fol - low you   as the years ____ go pass -

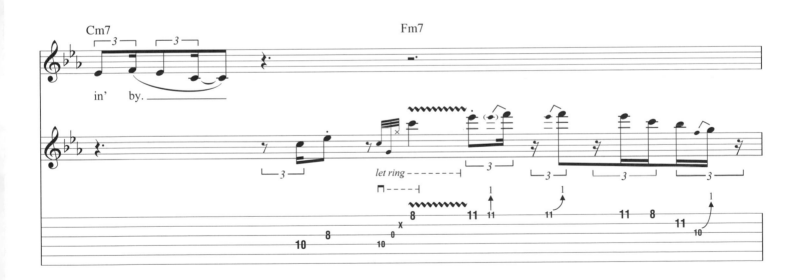

in' by. ____

Guitar Solo

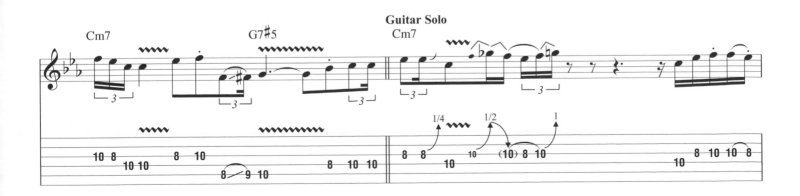

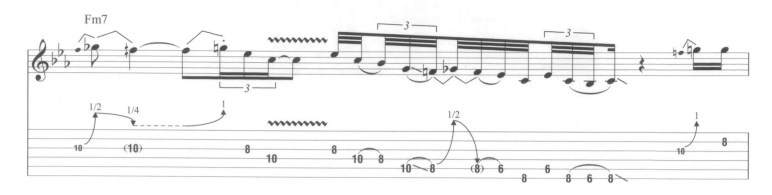

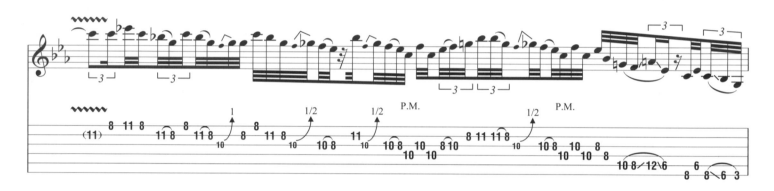

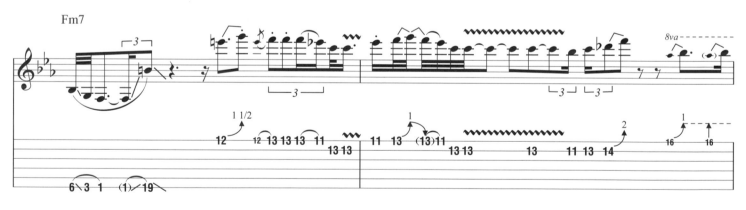

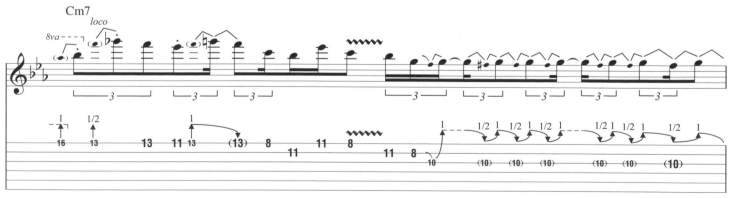

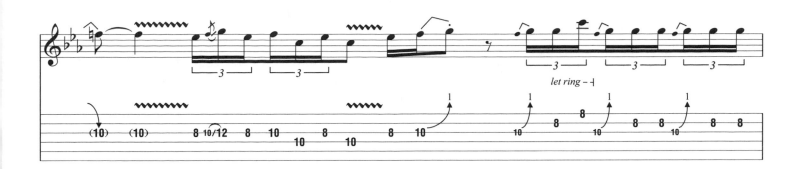

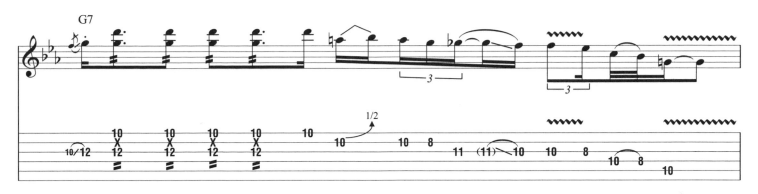

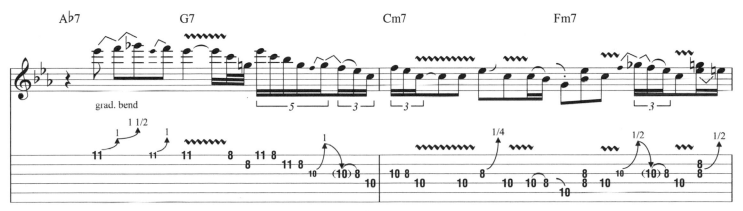

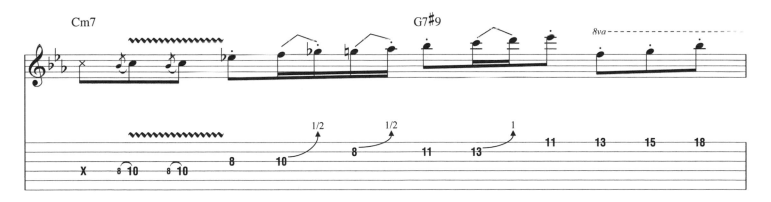

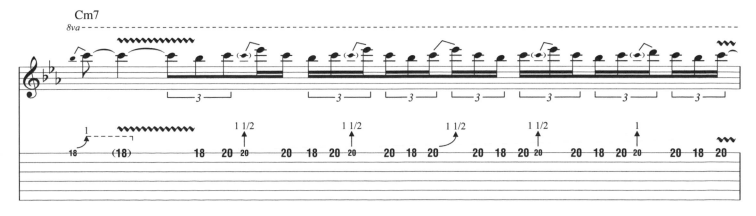

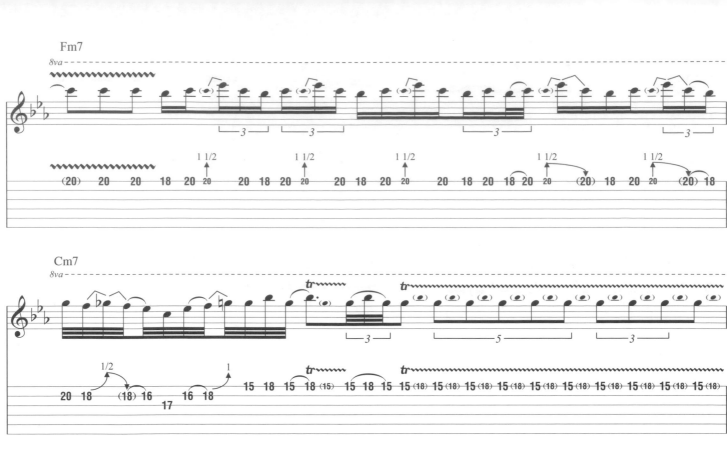

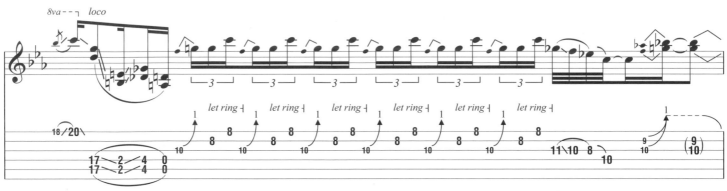

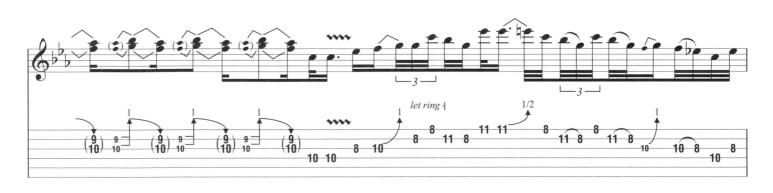

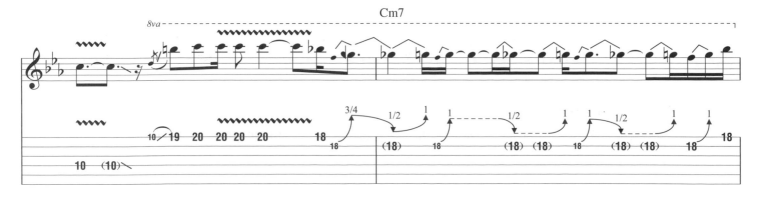

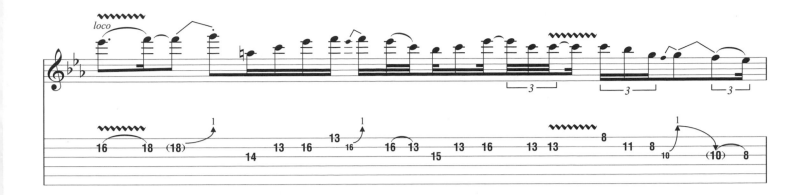

G7

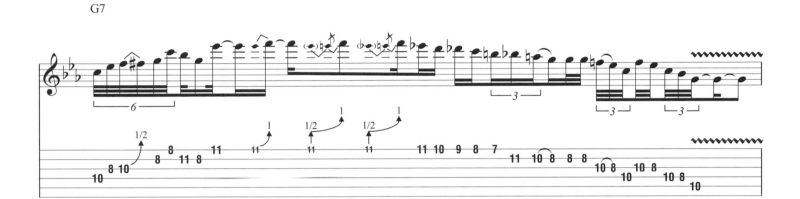

Ab7   G7

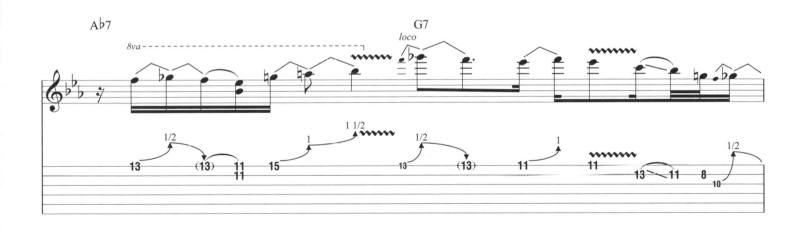

Cm7   Fm7

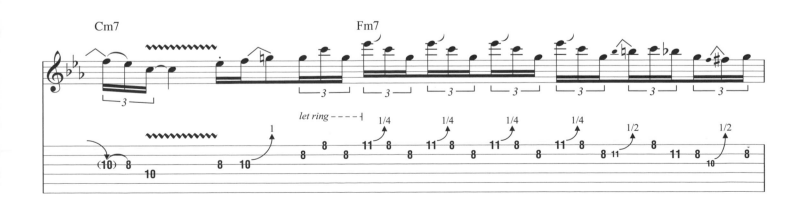

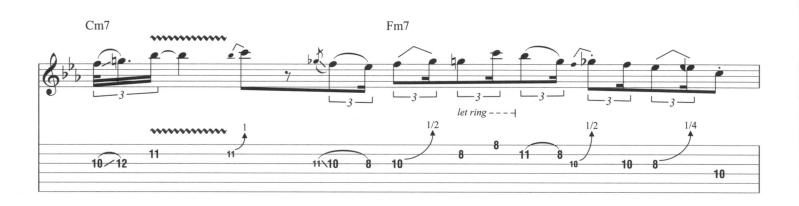

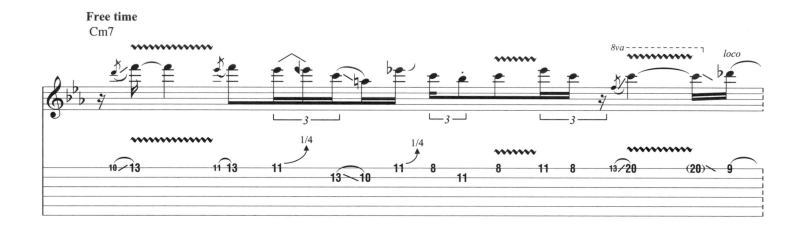

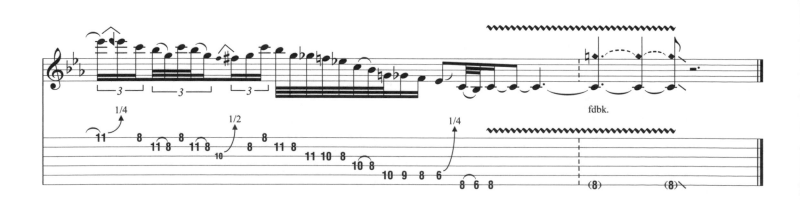

Cherry Red Wine

Words and Music by Luther Allison

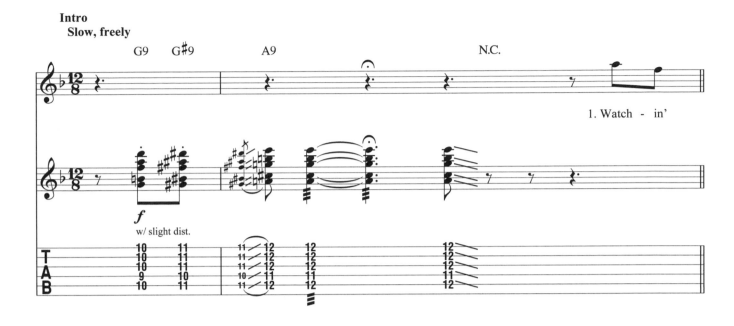

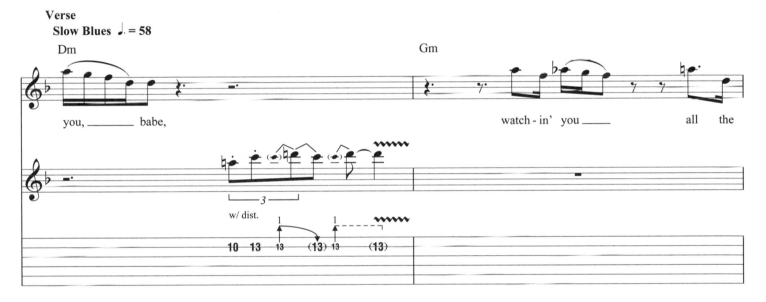

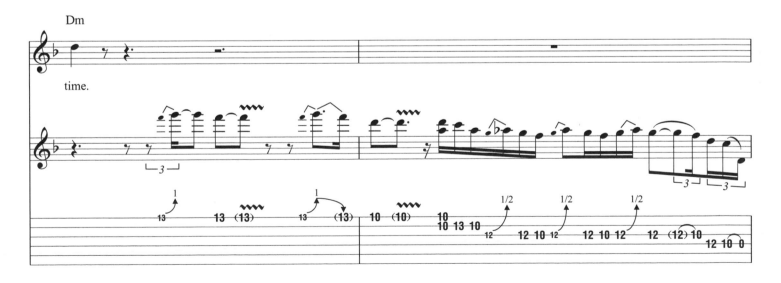

We've got so much to live for, ___ dar-lin',

but I just can't sit here ___ do-in' ___ noth-in' and

watch-in' that wine de-stroy ___ you.

Guitar Solo

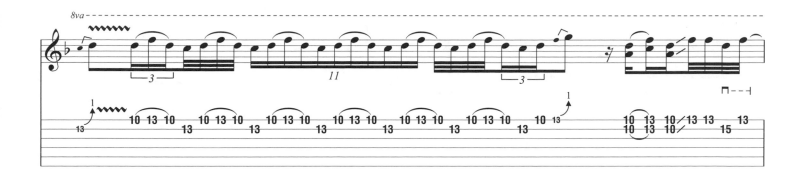

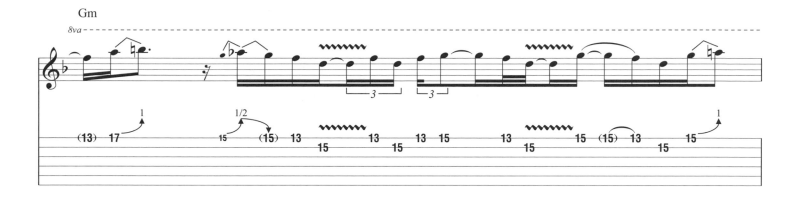

Gm

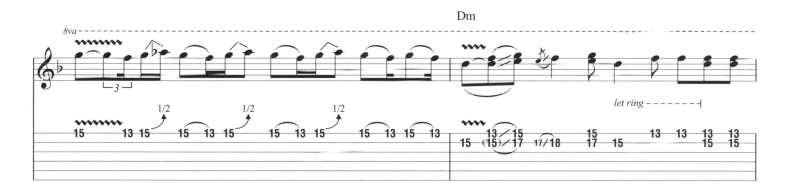

Dm

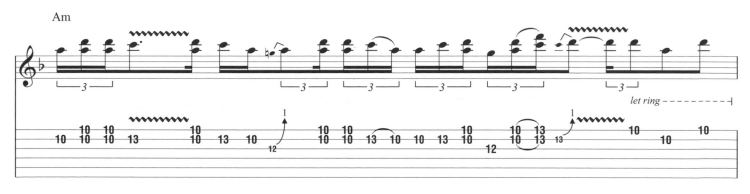

Am

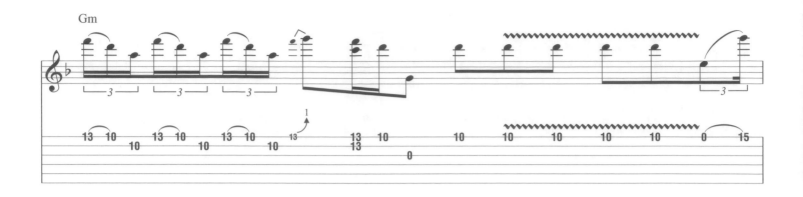

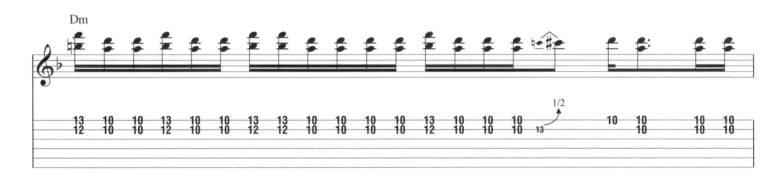

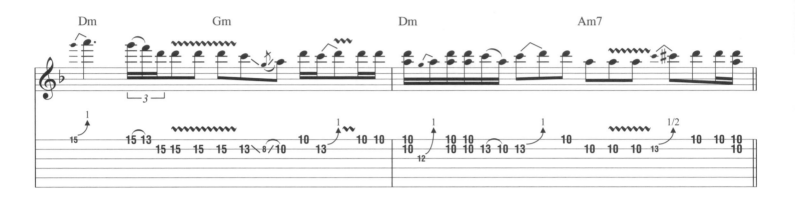

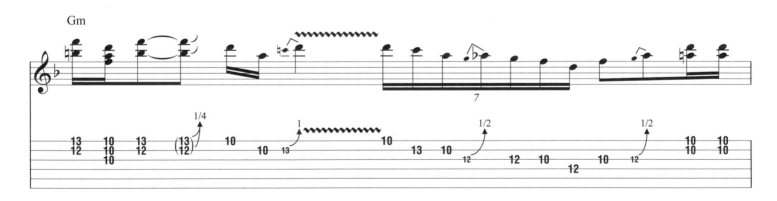

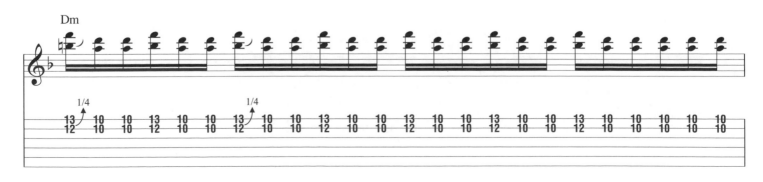

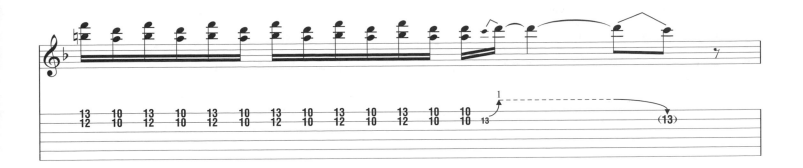

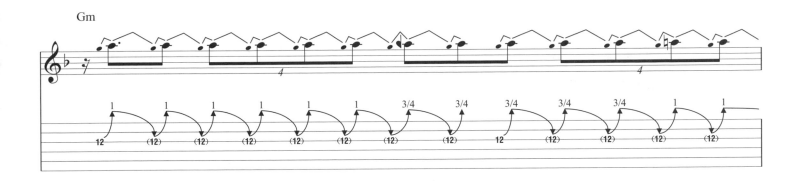

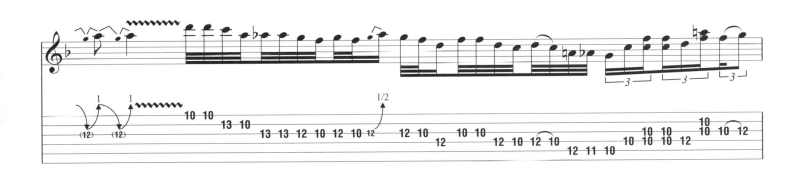

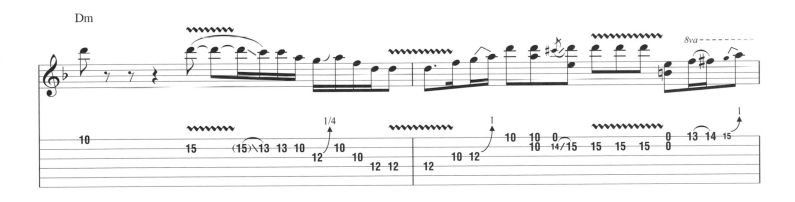

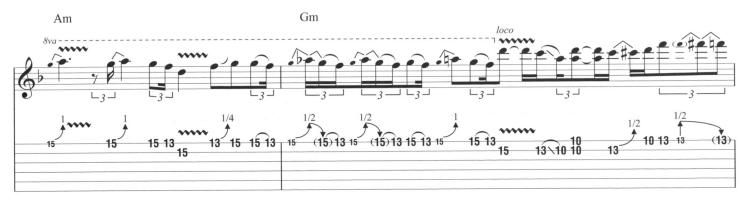

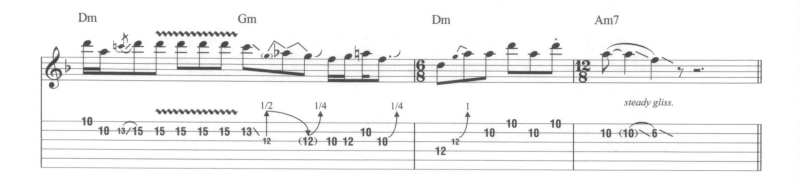

Verse

3. I'm tak-in' you to the doc-tor, dar-lin'.   May - be the doc-tor knows what's go-in' on in

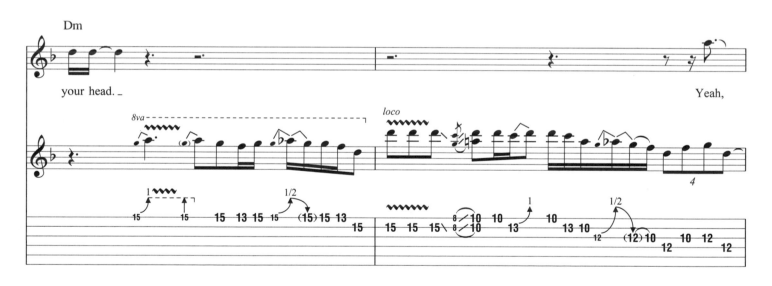

your head. _   Yeah,

I'm tak-in' you to the doc-tor, dar - lin'.

May-be he knows ___ what's go-in' ___ on in your head. ___

You're gon-na keep on drink-in' that bad ___ wine, ba-by,

Free time

e-ven the grass ___ that grows on your grave will be ___ cher-ry red. ___

A tempo

Free time

Double Trouble

Words and Music by Otis Rush

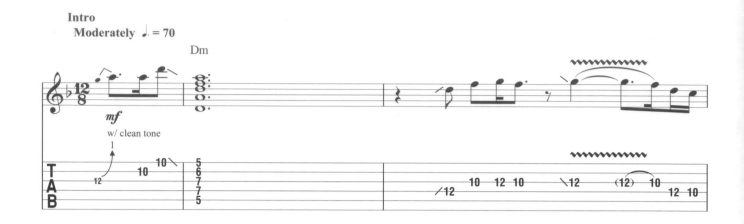

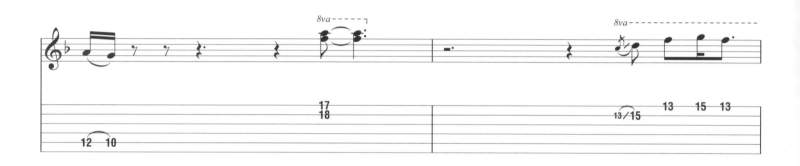

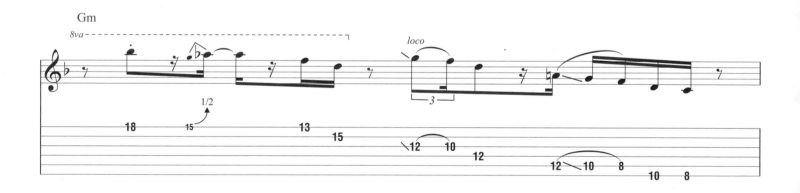

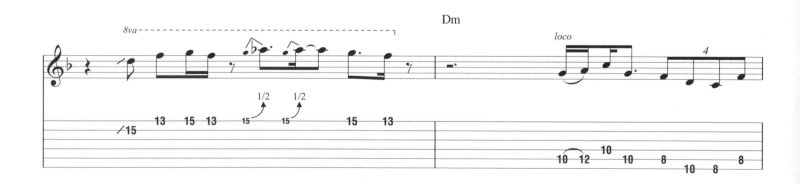

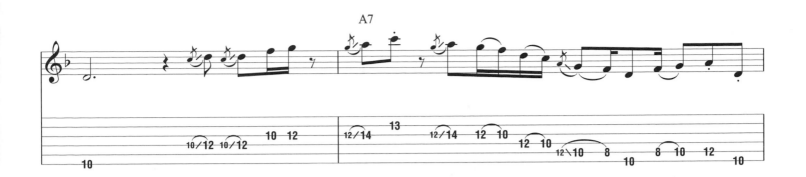

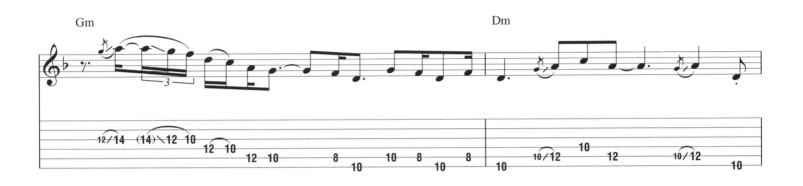

1. I'd lay a - wake at night, ___ these thoughts of love, ___ and just ___ so ___

trou - bled. ___ It's hard ___ to keep a job, ___ laid off and ___ hav - in' dou - ble

trou - ble. But, hey, hey, _____ yeah, __

they say you can make __ it if you try.

Yes, __ some of this gen - er - a - tion is mil - lion - air - es. __

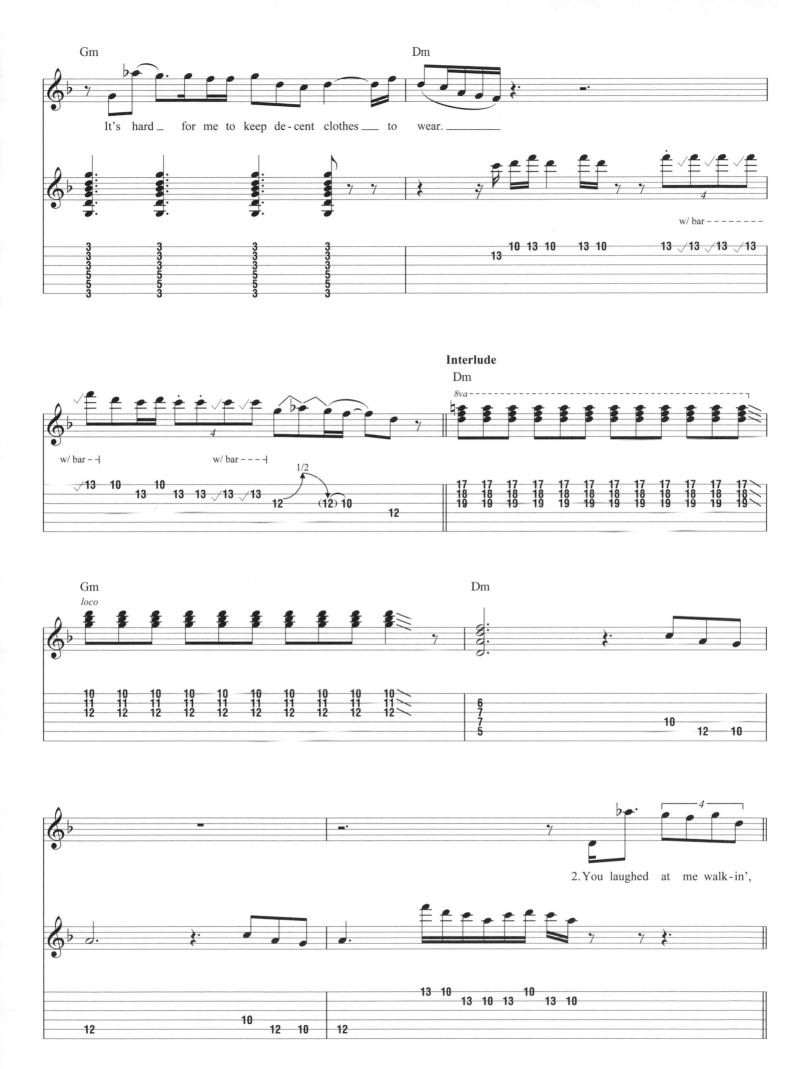

It's hard __ for me to keep de-cent clothes __ to wear. __

Interlude

2. You laughed at me walk-in',

Verse

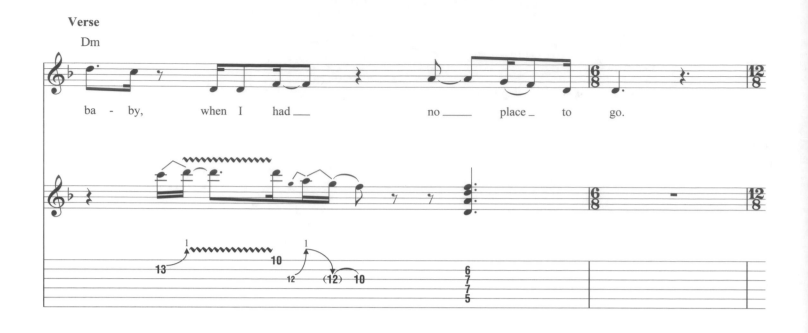

ba - by,   when I had ___   no ___ place ___ to   go.

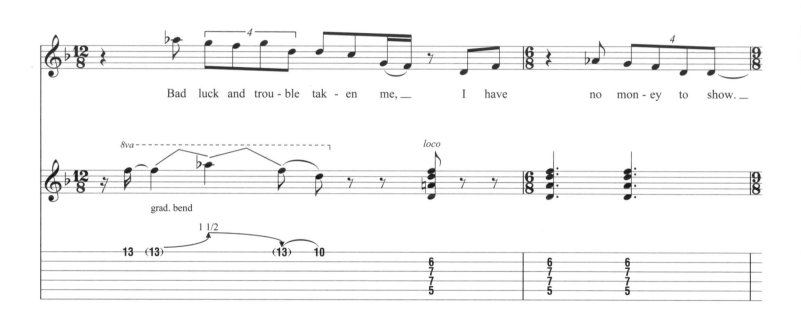

Bad luck and trou - ble tak - en me, ___   I have   no mon - ey to   show. ___

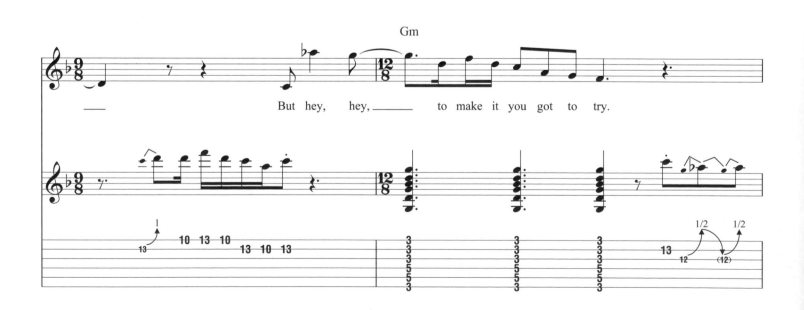

___   But hey,   hey, _____   to make it you got to   try.

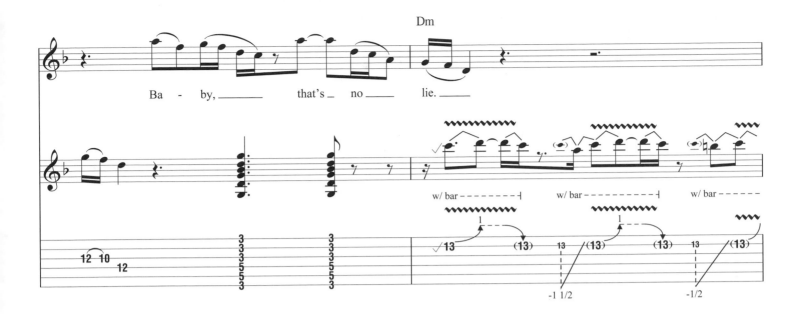

Ba - by, _____ that's _ no _____ lie. _____

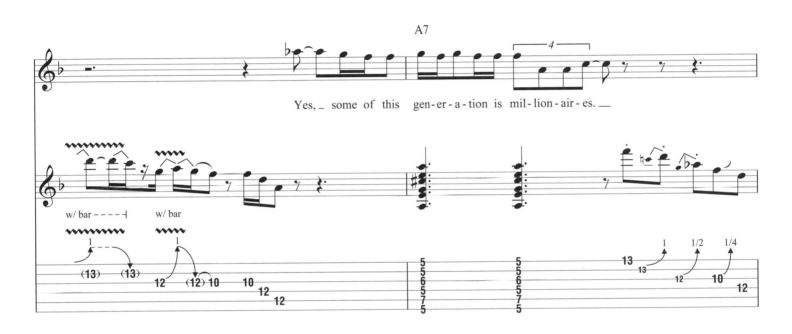

Yes, _ some of this gen-er-a-tion is mil-lion-air- es. _____

It's hard _____ for me to keep de - cent clothes _____ to

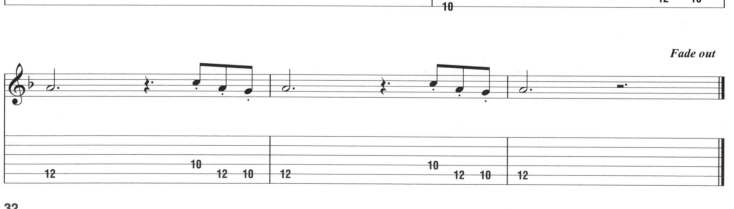

I Got a Mind to Give Up Living

By Nat Adderley

*Chord symbols reflect implied harmony.

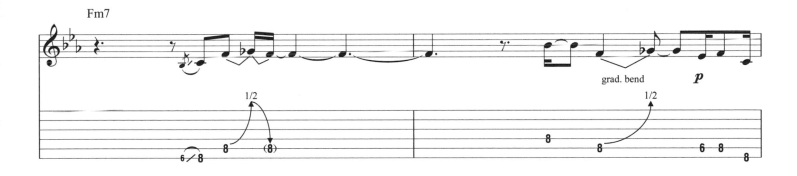

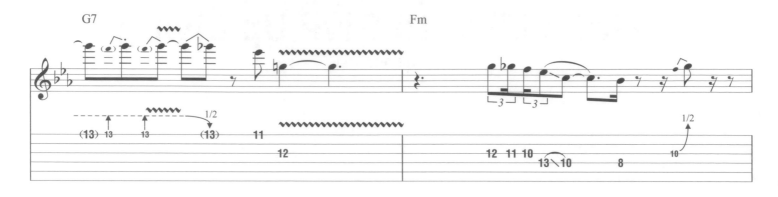

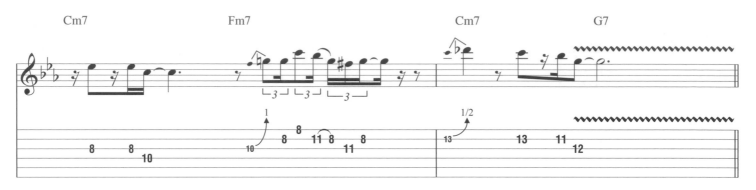

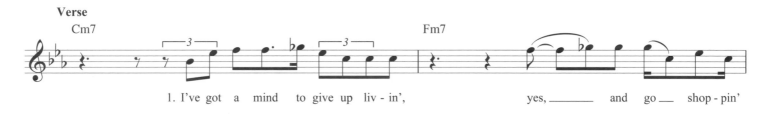

Verse

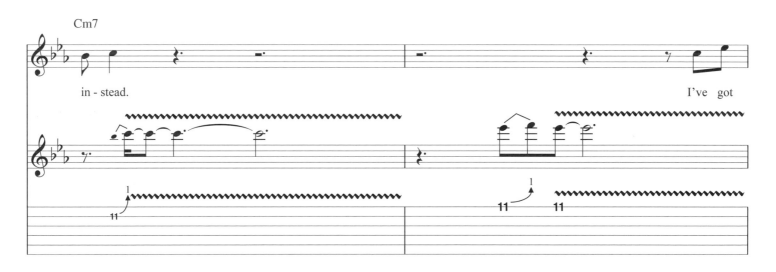

1. I've got a mind to give up liv-in', yes, _____ and go _____ shop-pin'

in - stead.   I've got

a mind _ to give up liv-in', yes, _____ and go shop-pin'

in - stead. _____

Pick me a tomb - stone _____ and be _____ pro - nounced _____ dead. _____

2. When I _____

Verse

_____ read your let - ter this morn - in' _____ that was on _____ your place _____ in _____

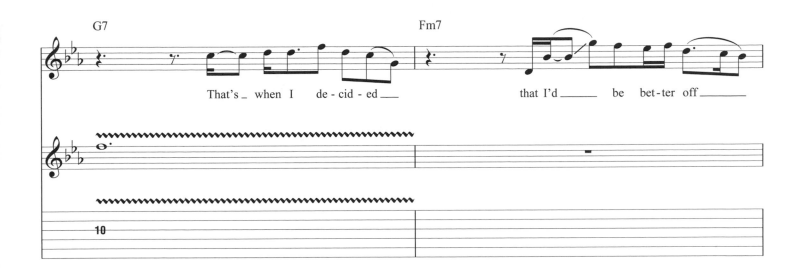

That's — when I de-cid-ed ___ that I'd _____ be bet-ter off _____

dead. _____   Oh, — yeah.

Guitar Solo

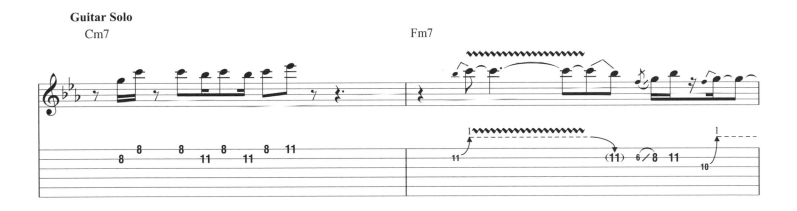

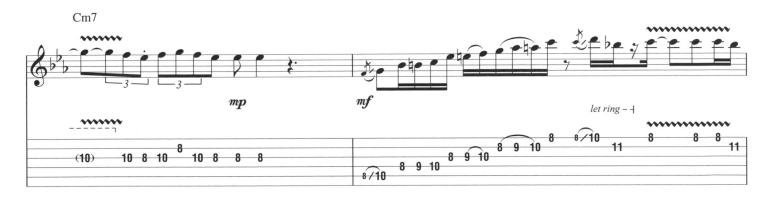

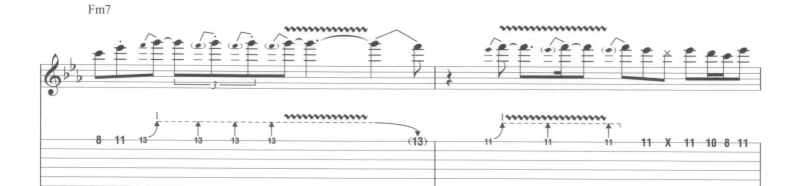

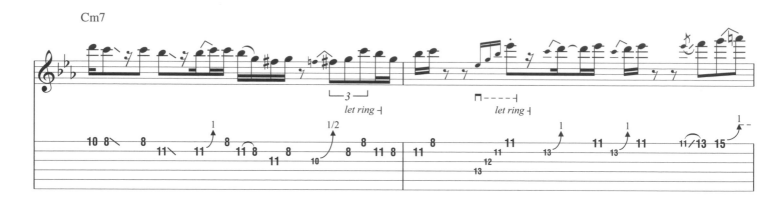

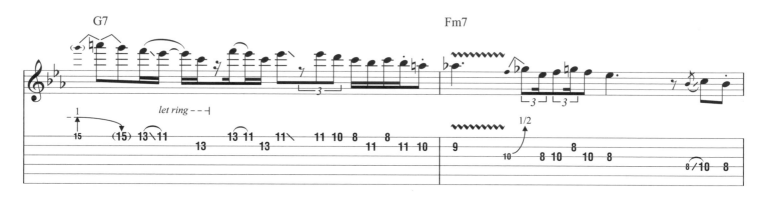

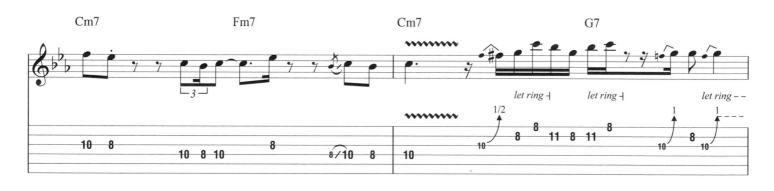

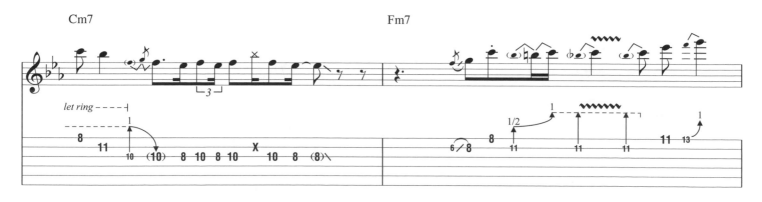

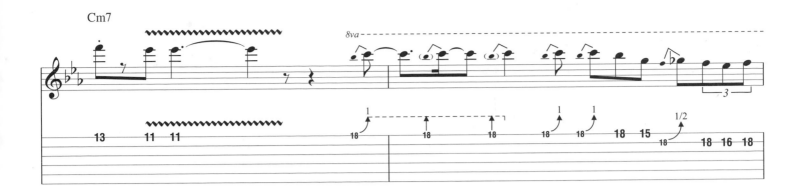

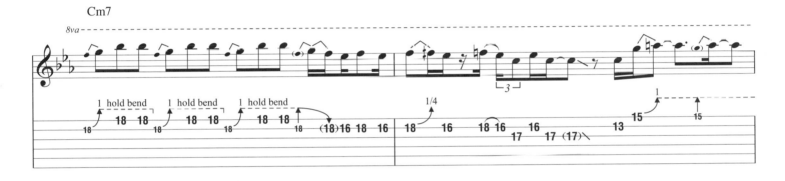

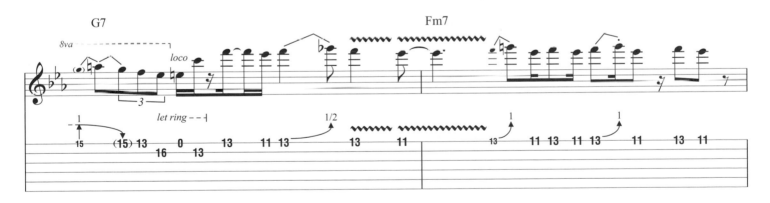

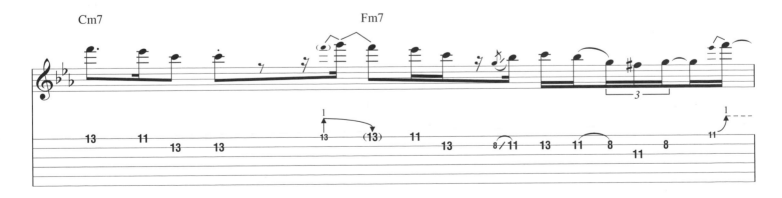

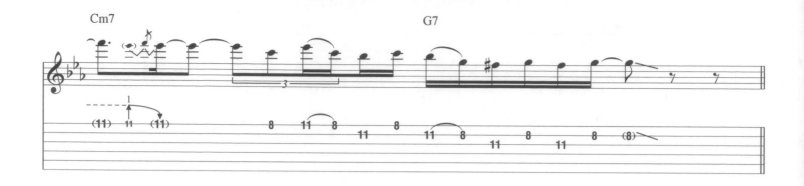

Verse

3. When I read __ your let - ter this morn - in' that was __ on __ your place __ in

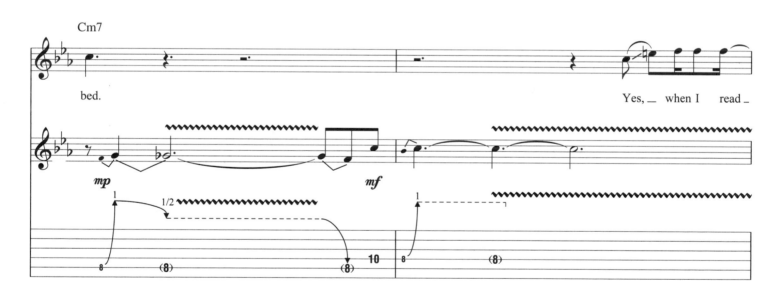

bed. Yes, __ when I read __

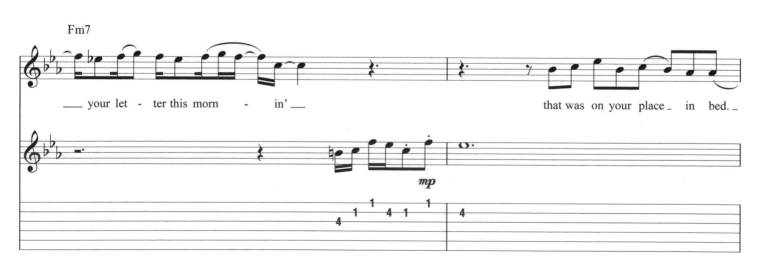

__ your let - ter this morn - in' __ that was on your place __ in bed. __

Be - cause

it's all ___ o - ver now ___ and ba - by you ___ can bet on

that. ___ Oh, ___ yeah. ___

Midnight Blues

Words and Music by Gary Moore

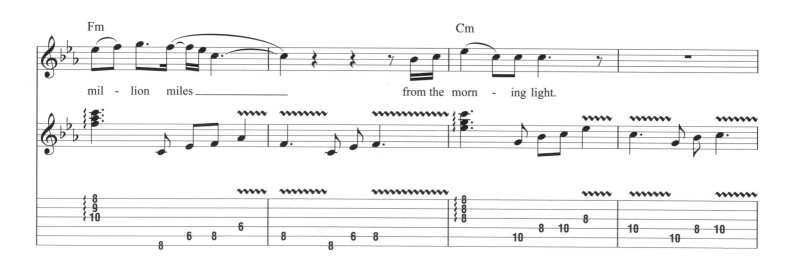

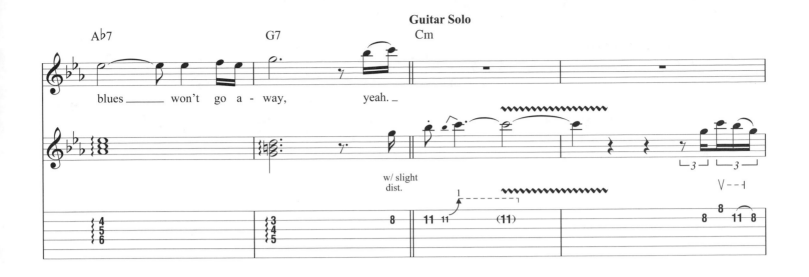

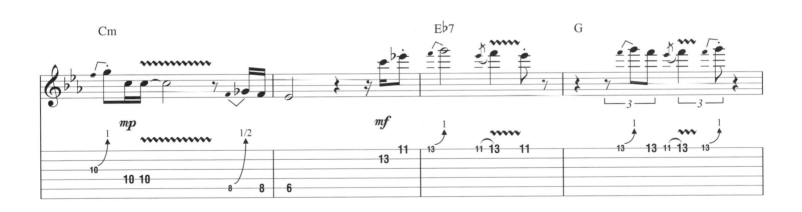

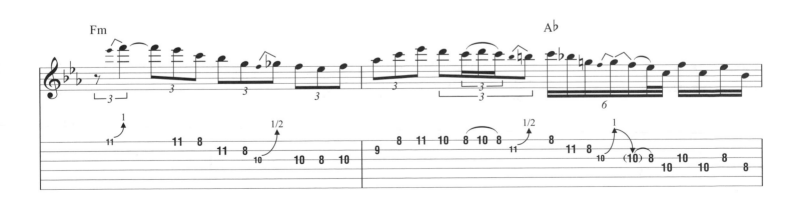

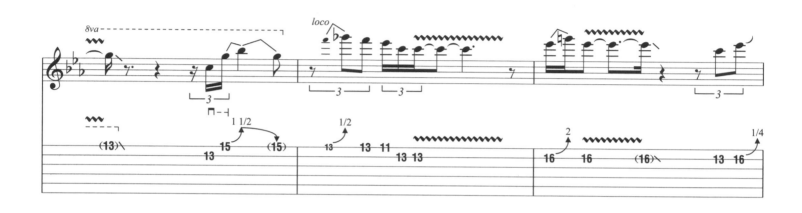

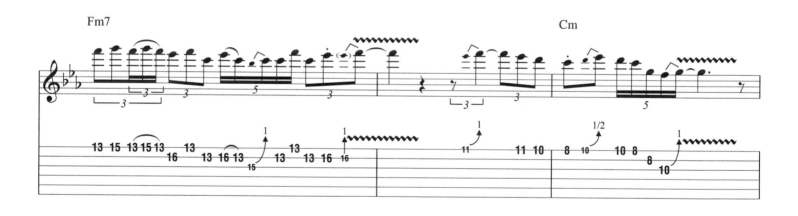

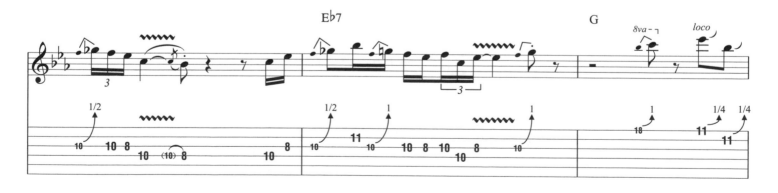

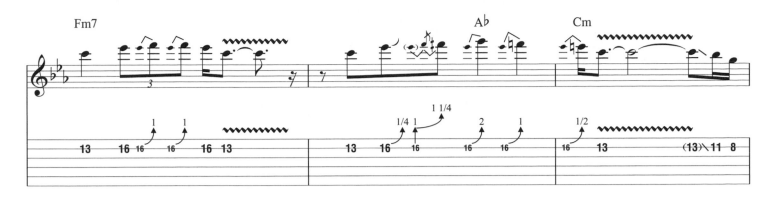

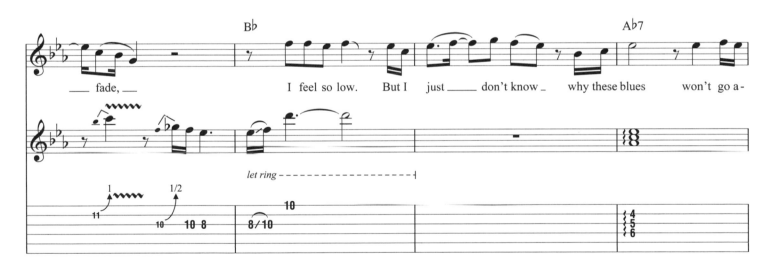

A Quitter Never Wins

Words and Music by Tinsley Ellis and Margaret Sampson

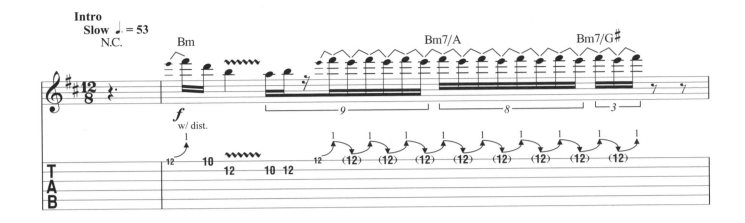

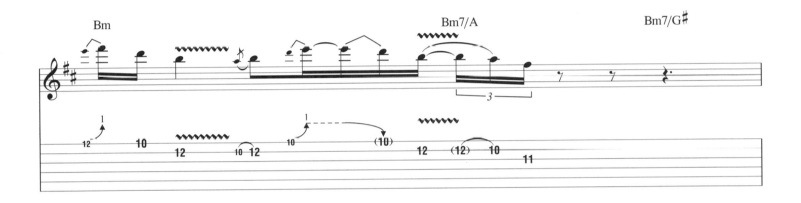

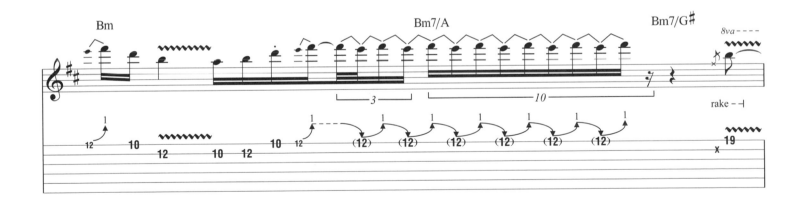

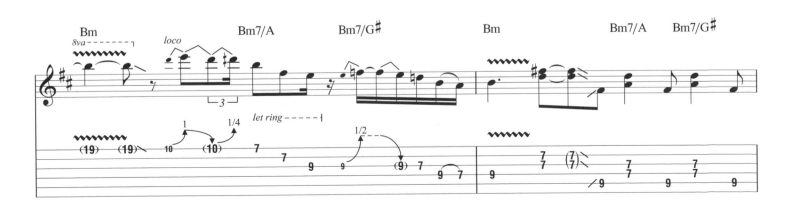

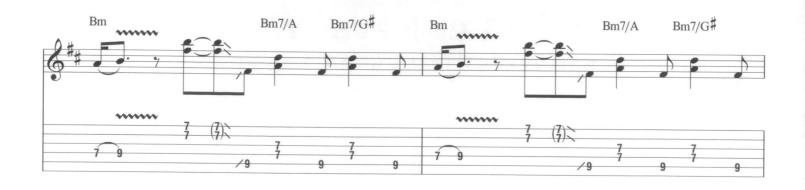

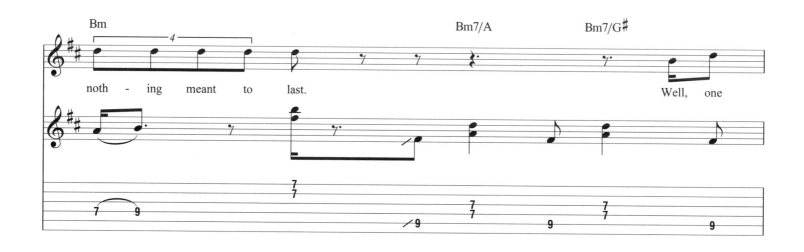

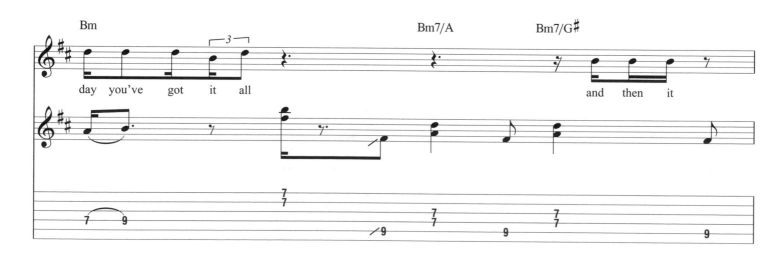

know   you   wan - na   quit   me,   ba - by,

ah,   but   a   quit-ter nev - er wins.

2. You've

Verse

walked   out   on   our _____   lov - ing   while   I

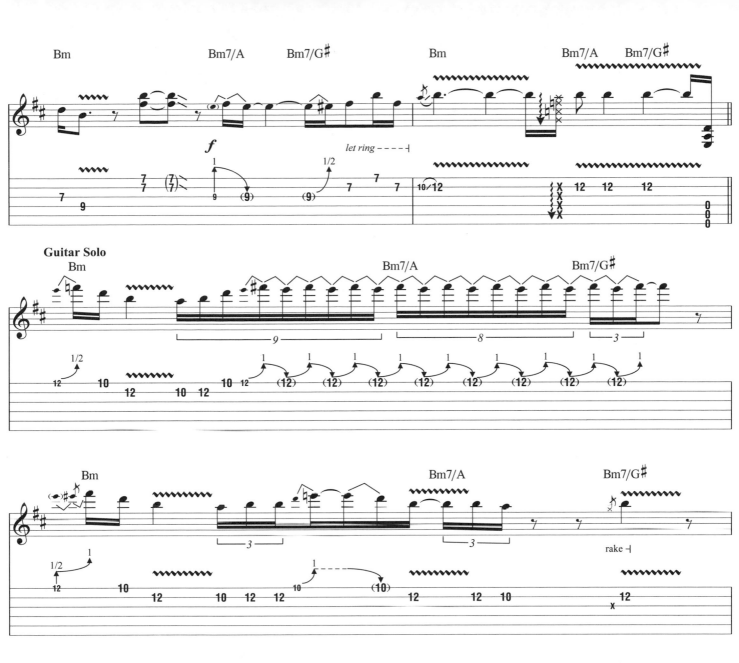

Guitar Solo

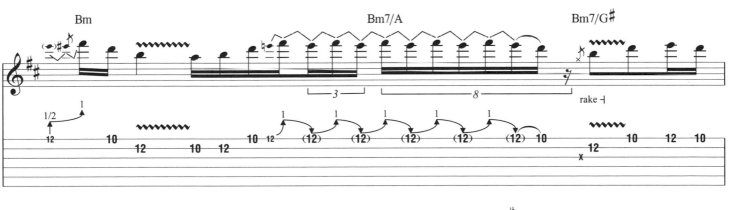

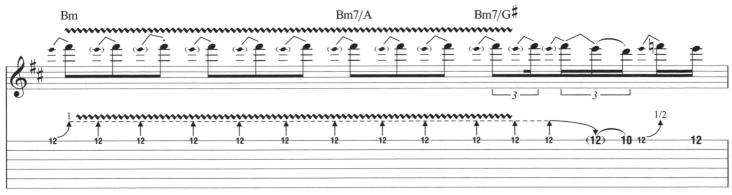

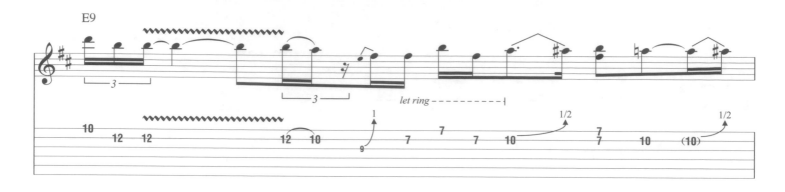

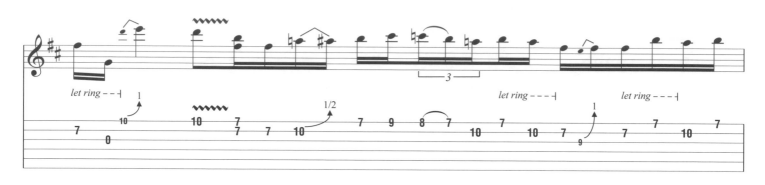

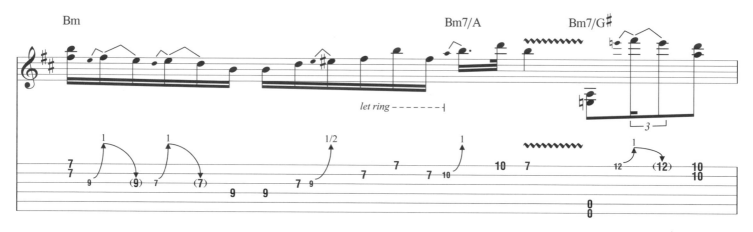

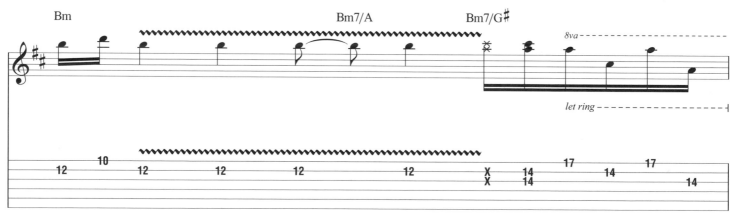

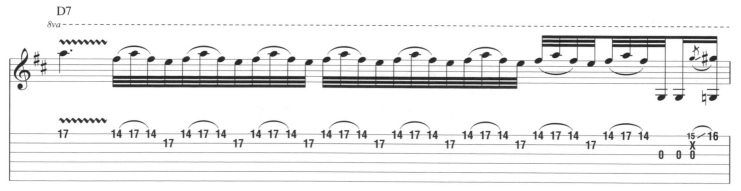

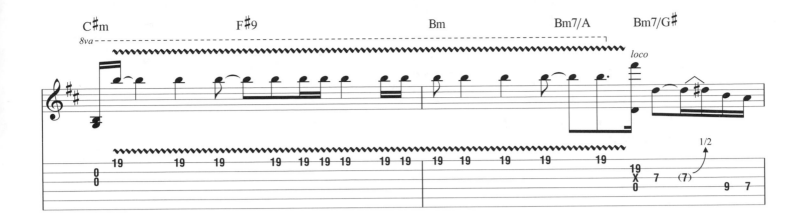

Piano Interlude

Gtr. tacet

Bm   Bm7/A Bm7/G#   Bm   Bm7/A Bm7/G#   Bm   Bm7/A Bm7/G#

3. It

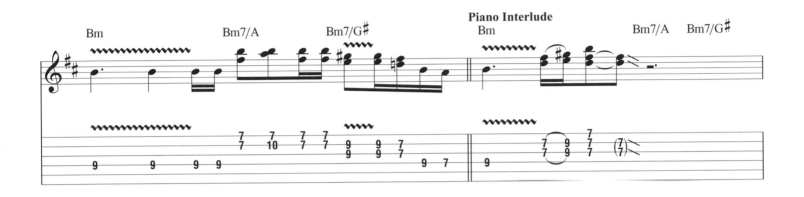

Verse

Bm   Bm7/A   Bm7/G#

seem   like   now - a - days   love's a

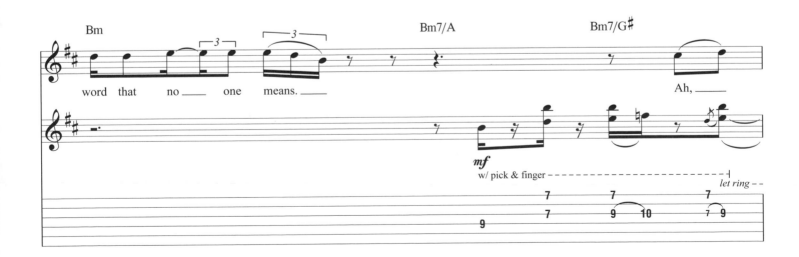

Bm   Bm7/A   Bm7/G#

word   that   no ____ one   means. ____   Ah, ____

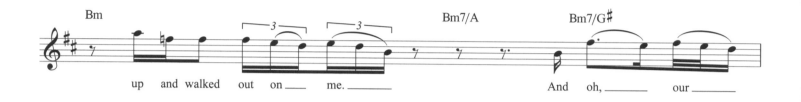

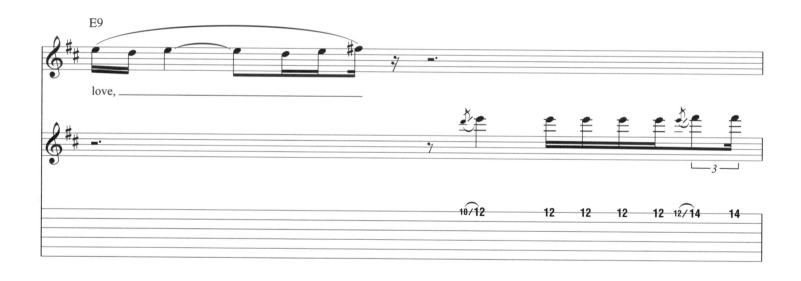

a - gain.

Well, I

know you wan - na quit me, ba - by, eh, yeah,

ha, but a, a quit - ter nev - er wins.

Guitar Solo

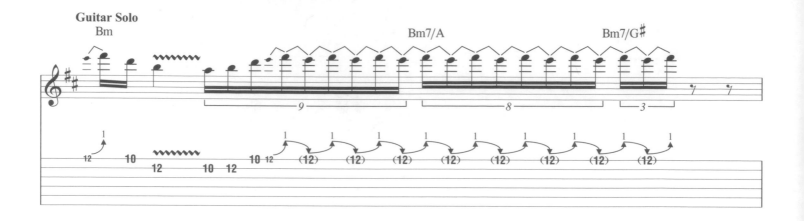

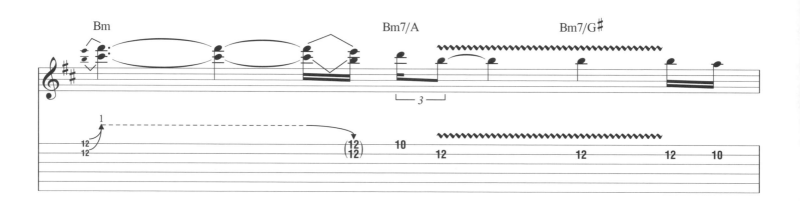

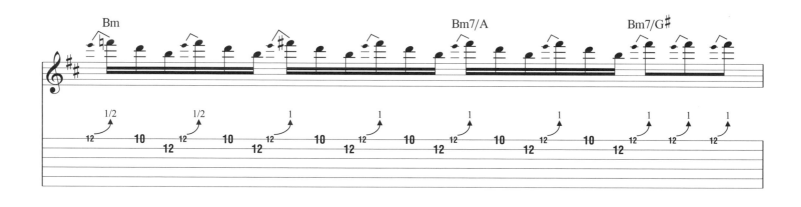

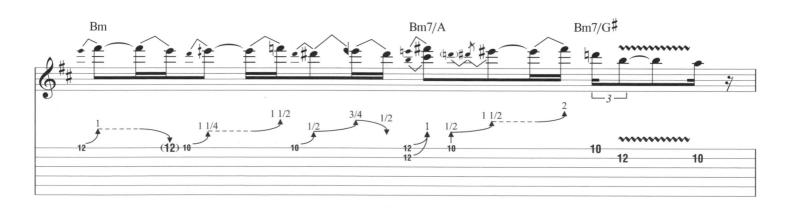

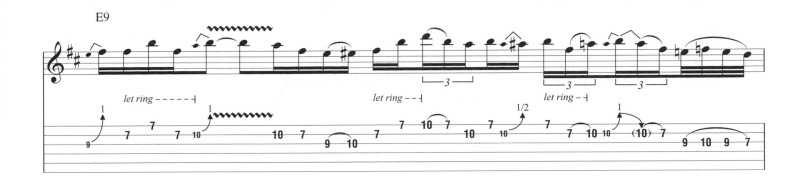

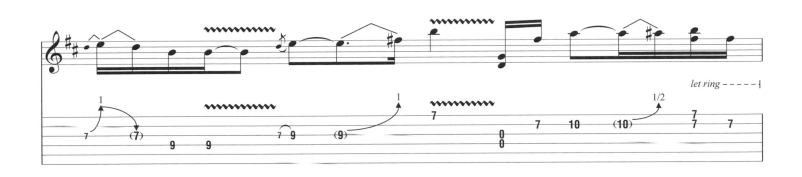

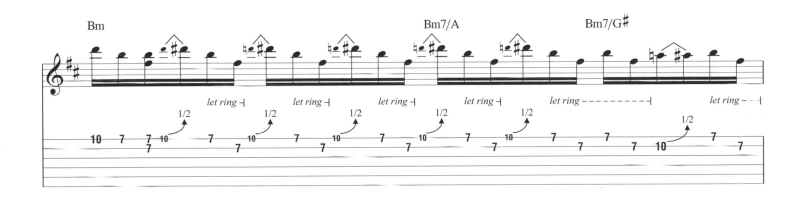

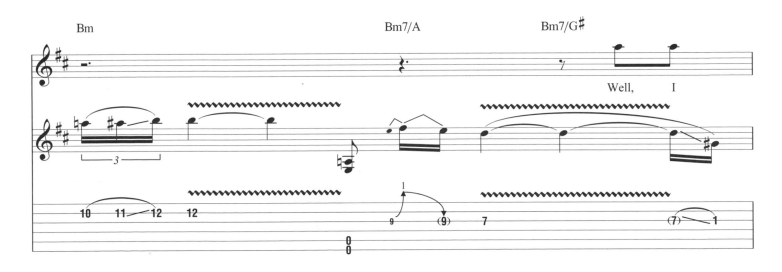

Gtr. tacet

D7

know you wan - na quit me, ba - by,

but a quit - ter nev - er wins, _____

a quit-ter nev - er

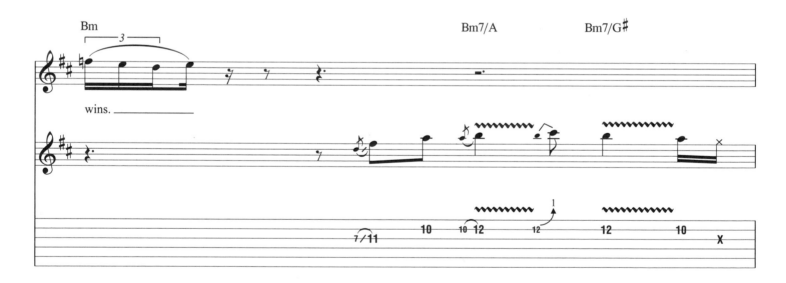

wins. _____

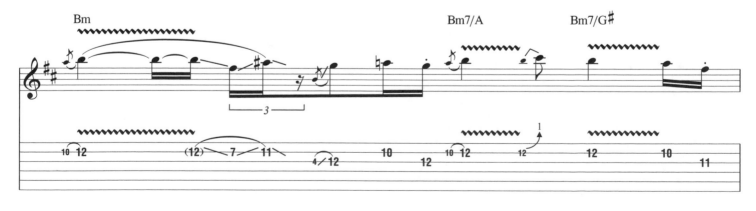

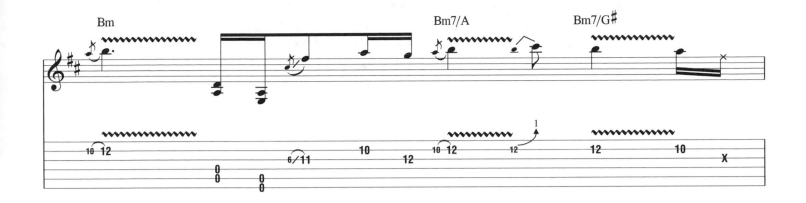

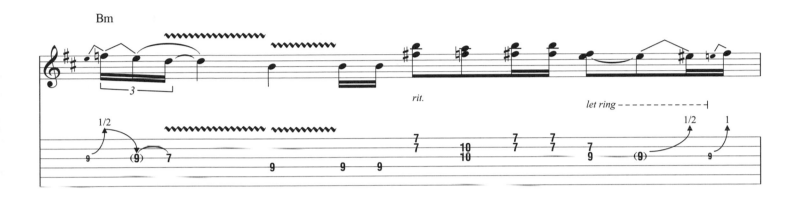

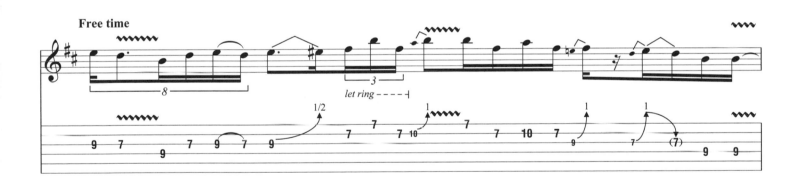

The Thrill Is Gone

Words and Music by Roy Hawkins and Rick Darnell

Intro
Moderately slow Blues ♩ = 88

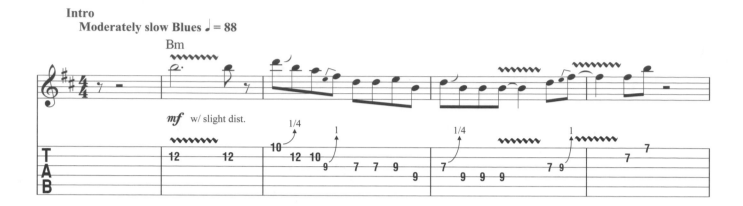

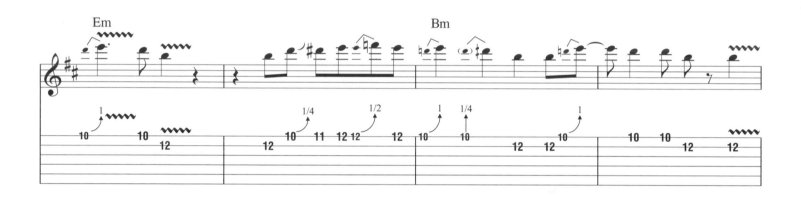

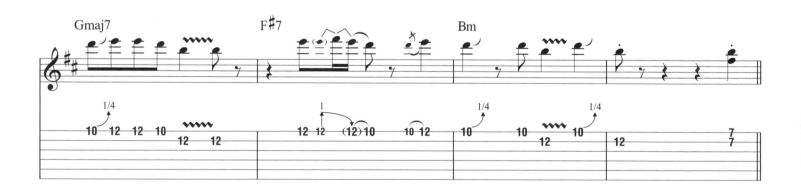

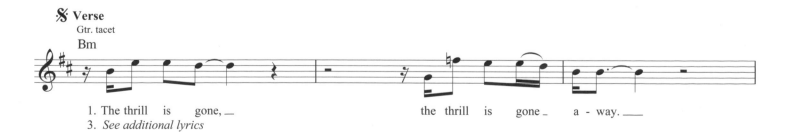

1. The thrill is gone, ___ the thrill is gone _ a - way. ___
3. *See additional lyrics*

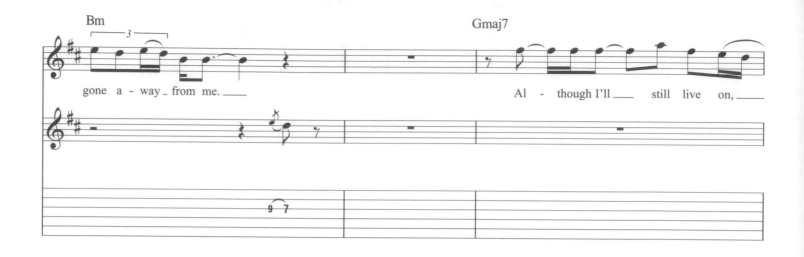

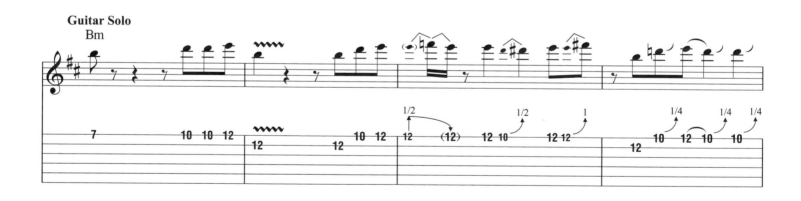

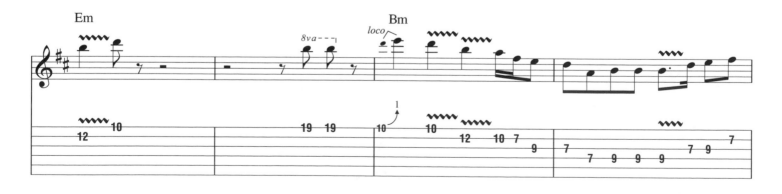

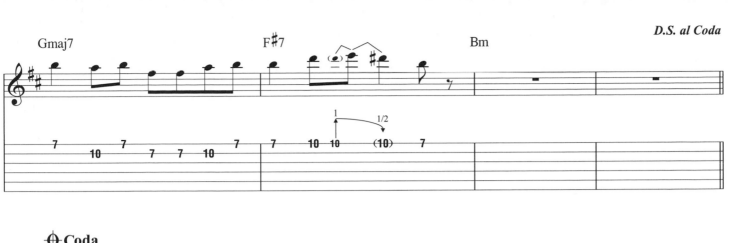

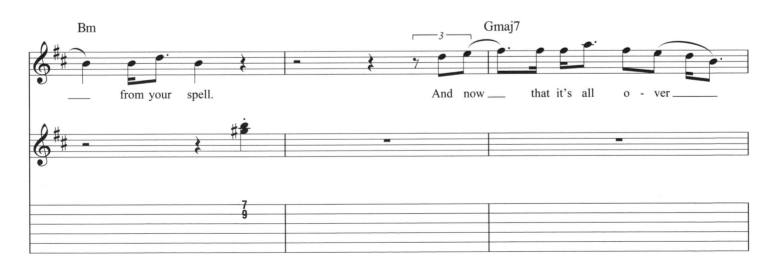

all I can do _____ is wish you ____ well. _____

Outro-Guitar Solo

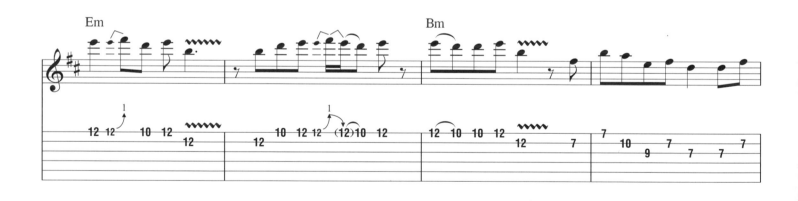

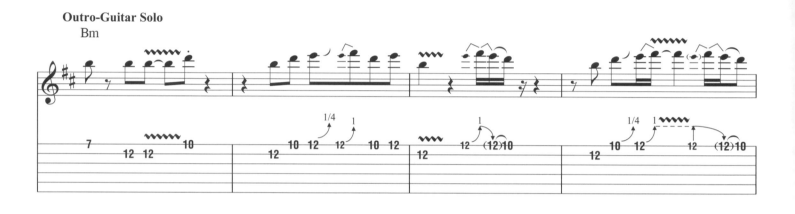

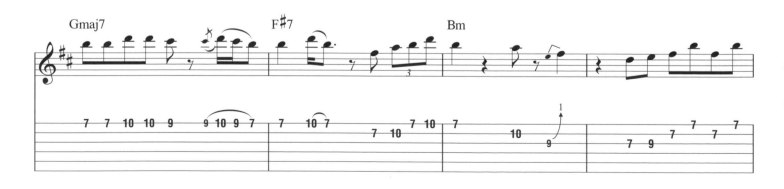

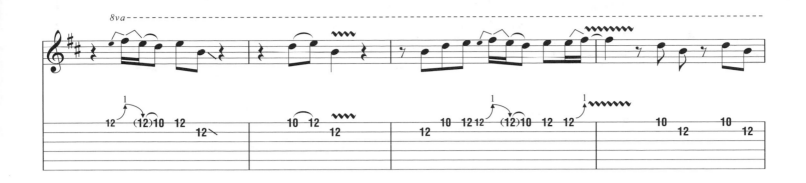

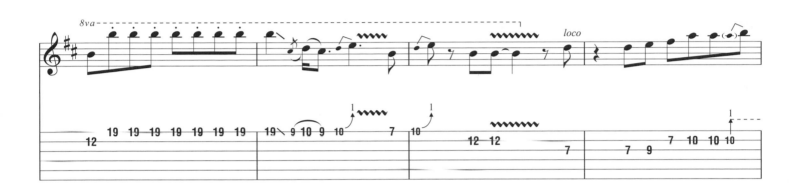

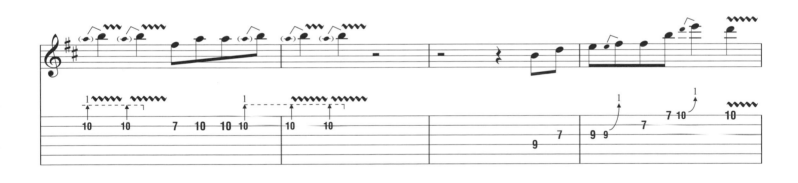

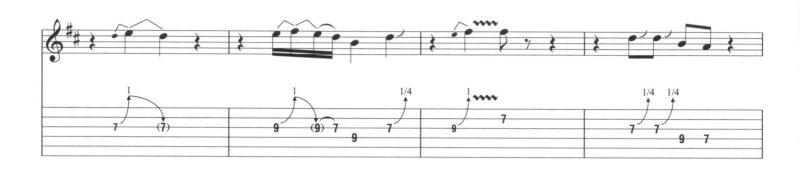

Begin fade

Fade out

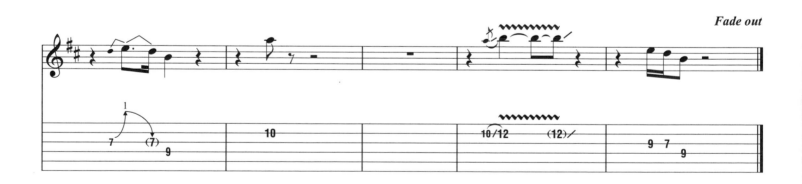

Additional Lyrics

3. The thrill is gone,
It's gone away for good.
Oh, the thrill is gone,
Baby, it's gone away for good.
Someday I know I'll be holdin' on, baby,
Just like I know a good man should.

Tin Pan Alley

Words and Music by Robert Geddins

Tune down 1/2 step:
(low to high) Eb-Ab-Db-Gb-Bb-Eb

Intro
Slow Blues ♩ = 40

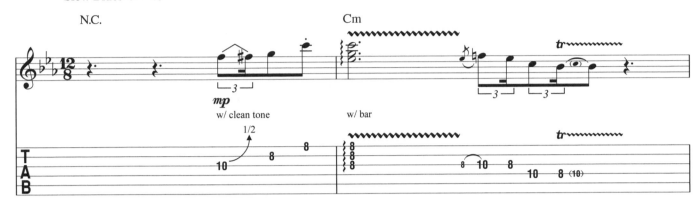

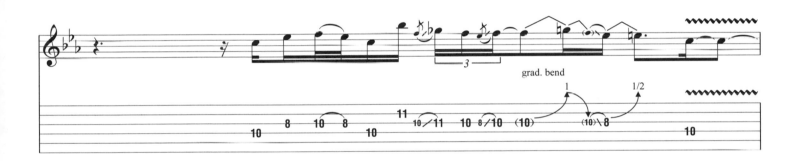

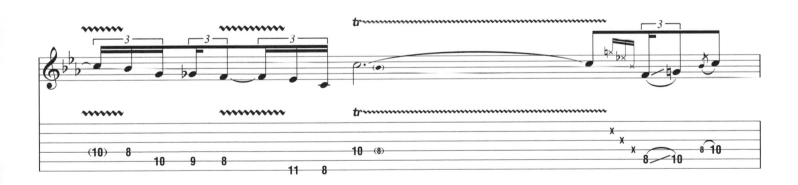

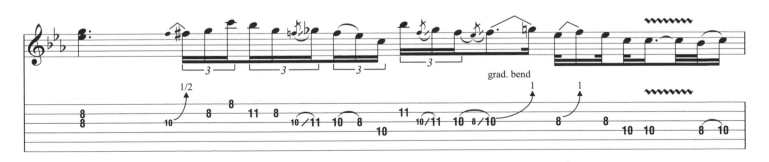

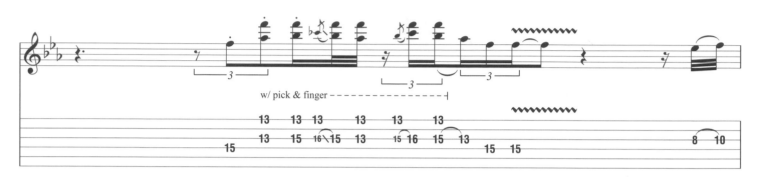

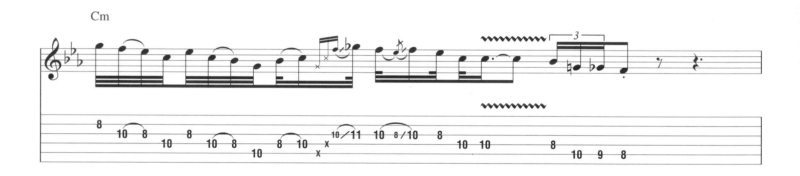

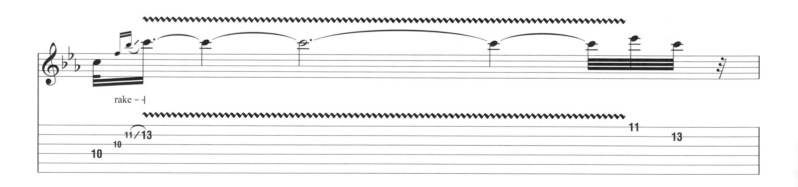

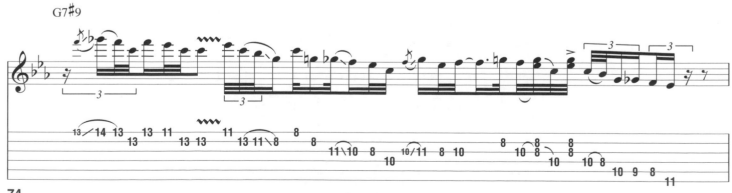

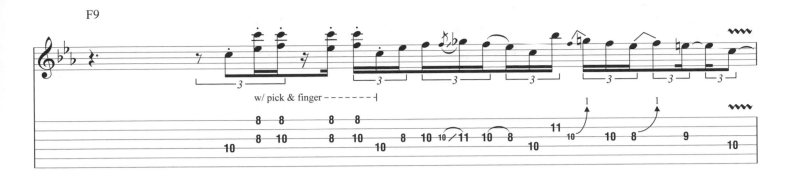

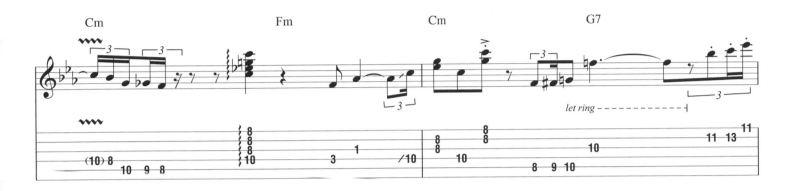

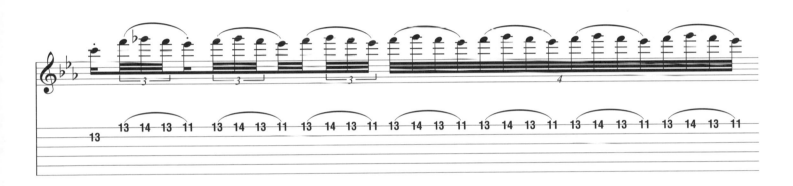

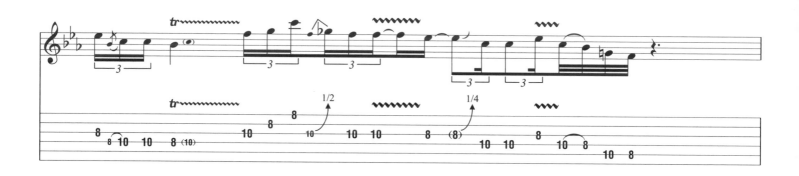

F9

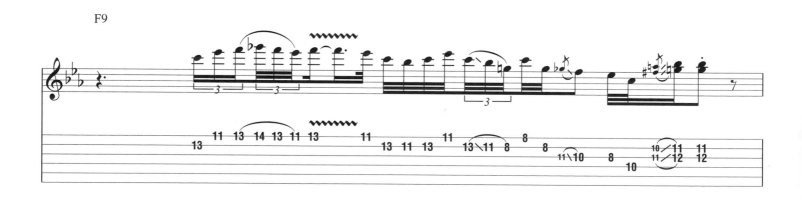

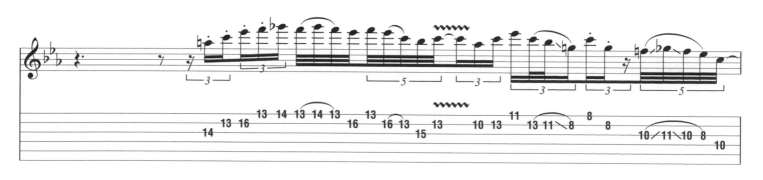

Cm

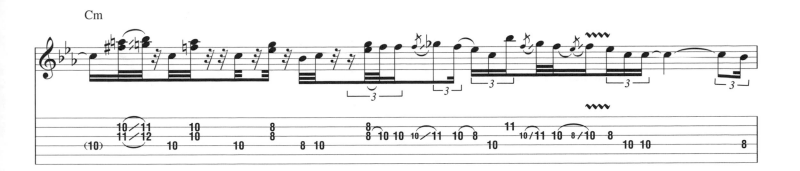

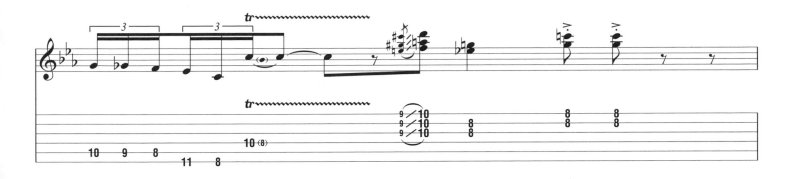

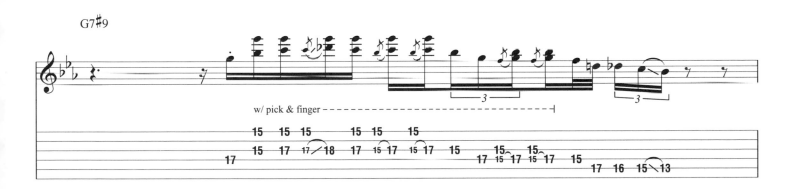

G7#9

Fm

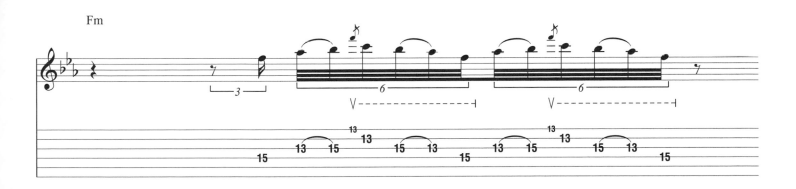

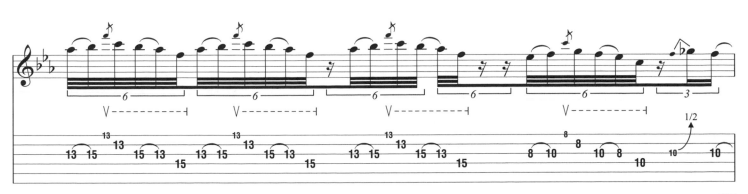

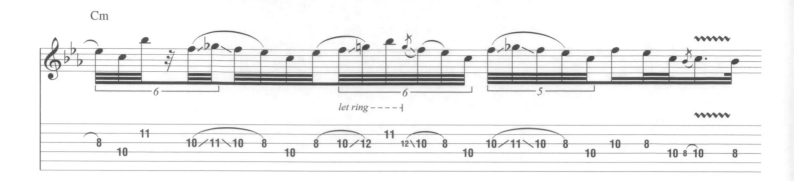

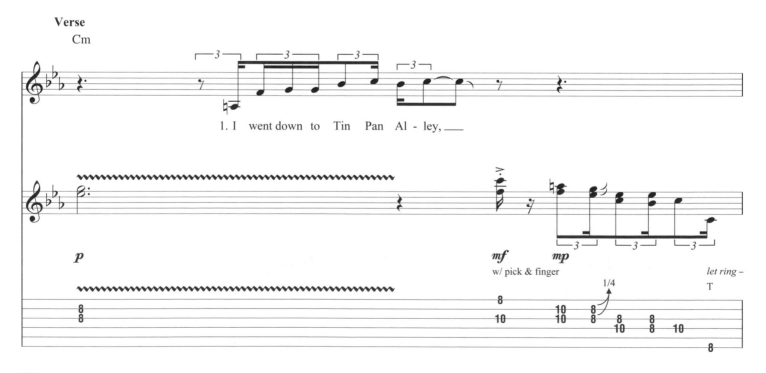

see ___ what was go - in' on.

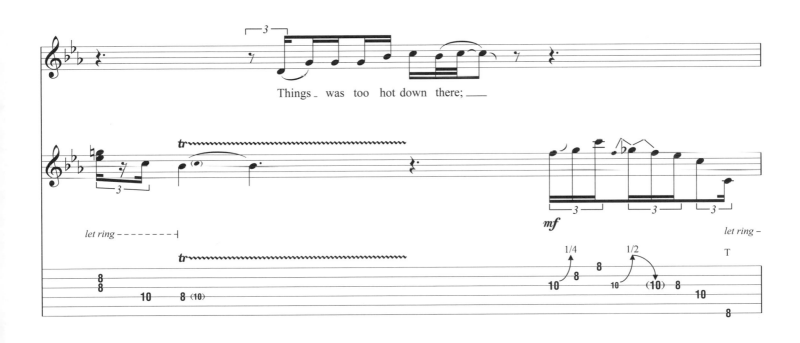

Things ___ was too hot down there; ___

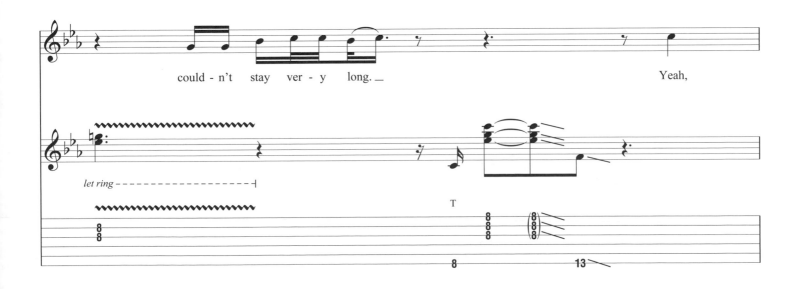

could - n't stay ver - y long. ___ Yeah,

All ___ the peo - ple down there ___

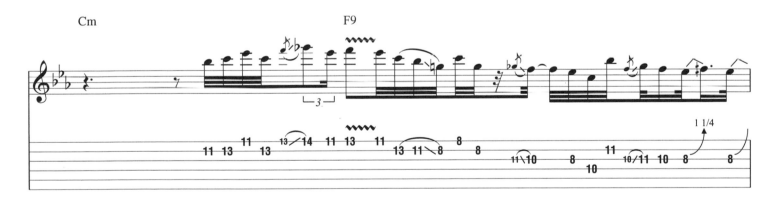

liv - in' for their whis - key, wine 'n' gin. ___

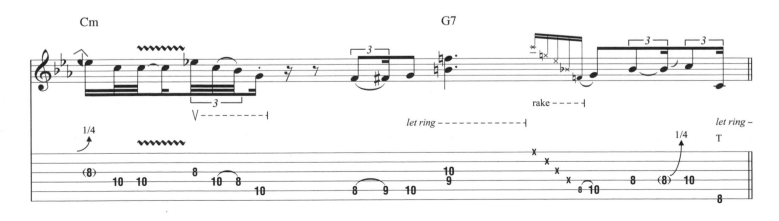

Verse

Cm

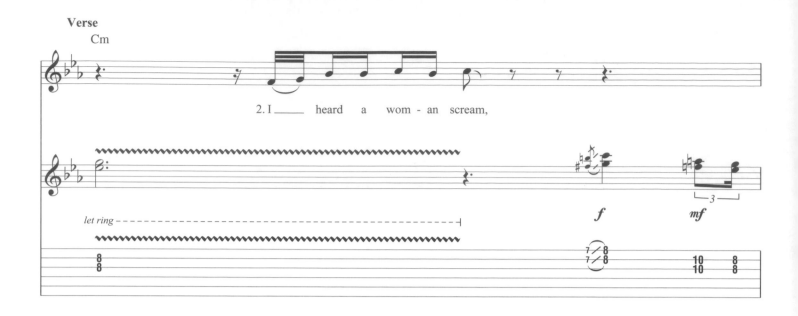

2. I ___ heard a wom - an scream,

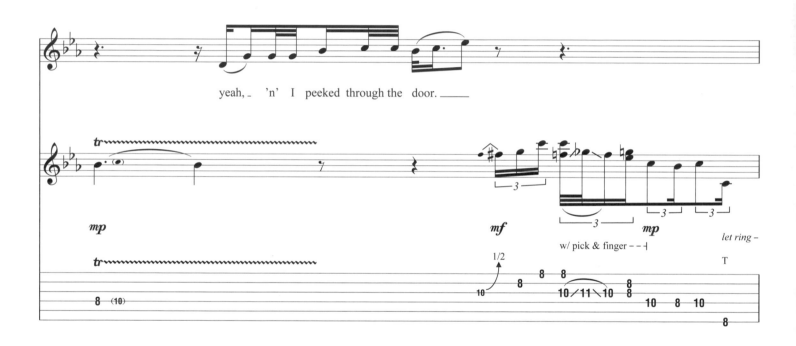

yeah, ___ 'n' I peeked through the door. ___

Some cat was work-in' on An-nie with a

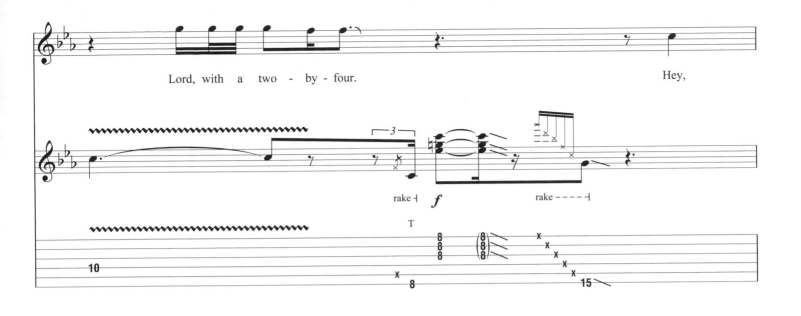

Lord, with a two - by - four.   Hey,

Fm

hey,

al - ley's the rough - est place   I've   ev - er

been.

All the peo-ple down there, ___

liv - in' for their whis - key, ___ wine 'n' gin.

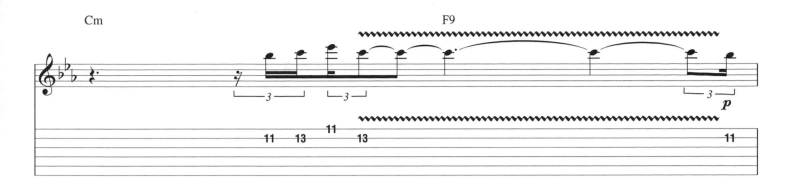

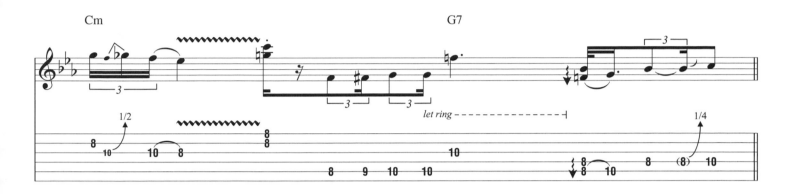

Verse

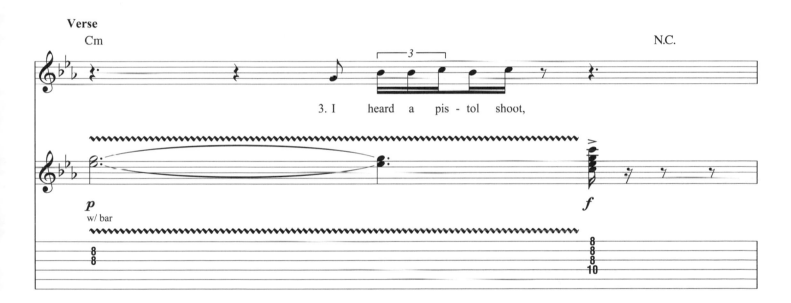

3. I heard a pis-tol shoot,

yeah, __ 'n' it was a for-ty-four.

Some - bod - y killed a crap shoot-er 'cause he did-n't

shake, _____ rat - tle 'n' roll. Hey, _____

hey, _____

Fm

al - ley's the rough - est place I've ev - er

been.

All __ the peo - ple down there __

*Snap string w/ middle finger.

87

kill - in' for their whis - key___ wine 'n' gin. _____

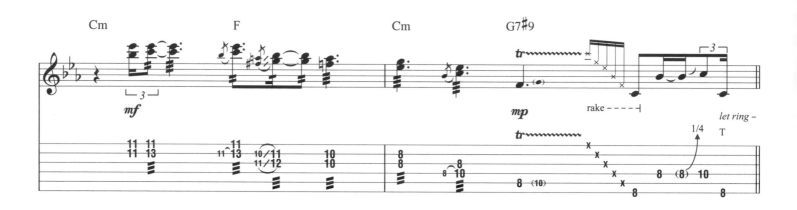

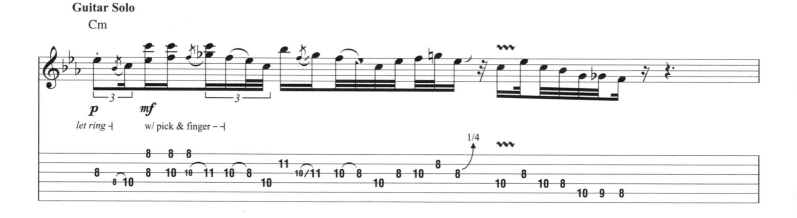

Guitar Solo

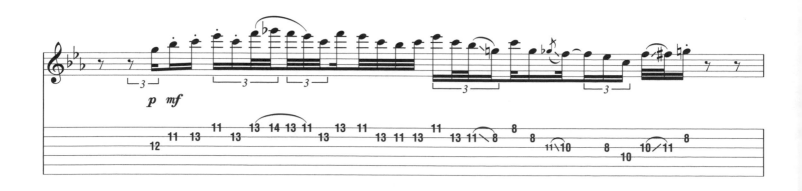

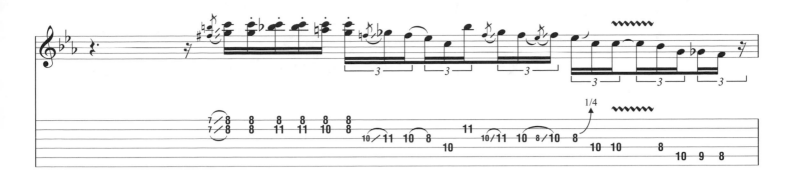

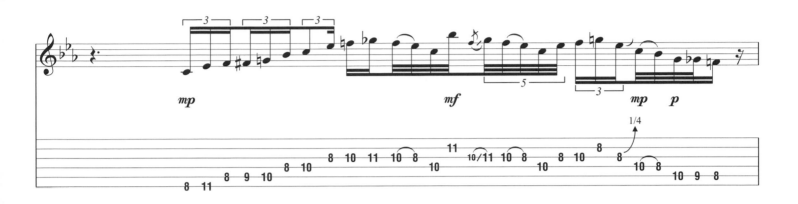

F9

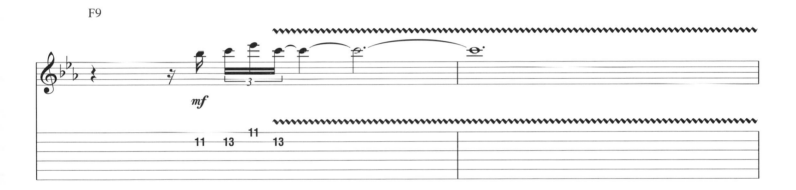

Cm

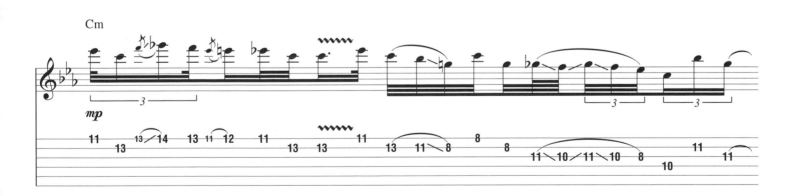

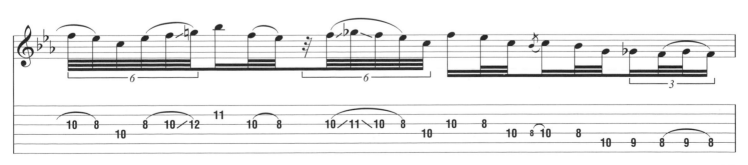

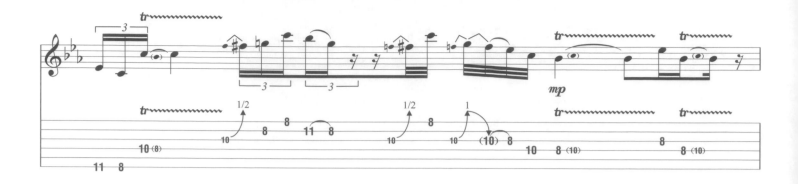

Gm

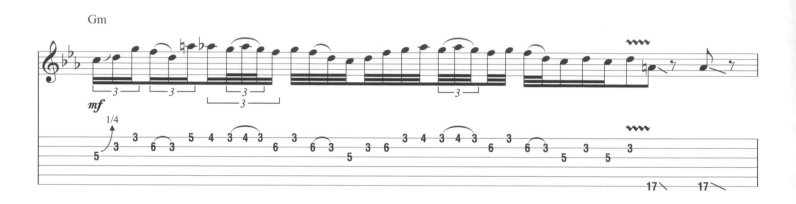

Fm

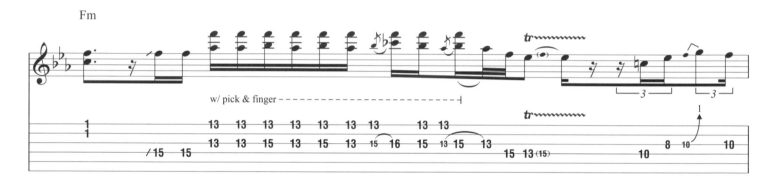

Cm   F9

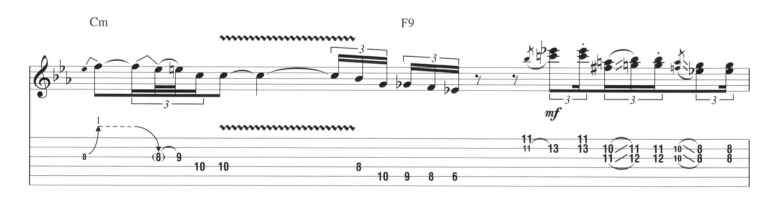

Cm   G7

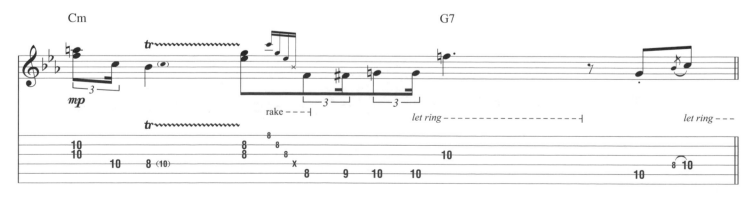

90

Verse

Cm

4. I hear a cop, stand-ing

with his hand on his gun, _

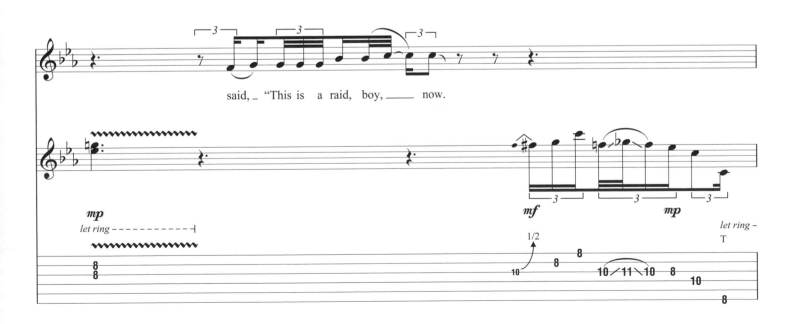

said, _ "This is a raid, boy, _____ now.

Lord, ___ no - bod - y run!" Hey, ___

let ring - - - - - - - - - - - -

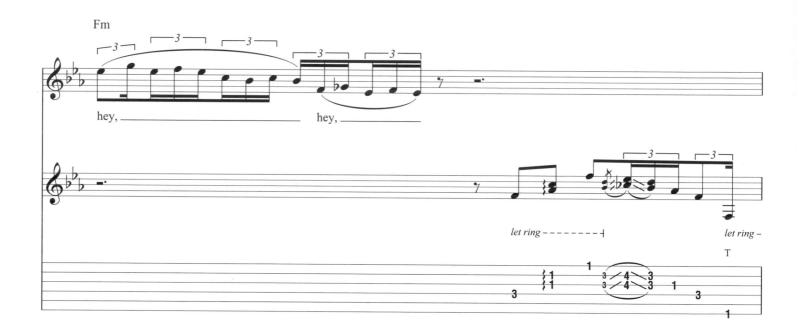

Fm

hey, ___ hey, ___

let ring - - - - - -

let ring -

T

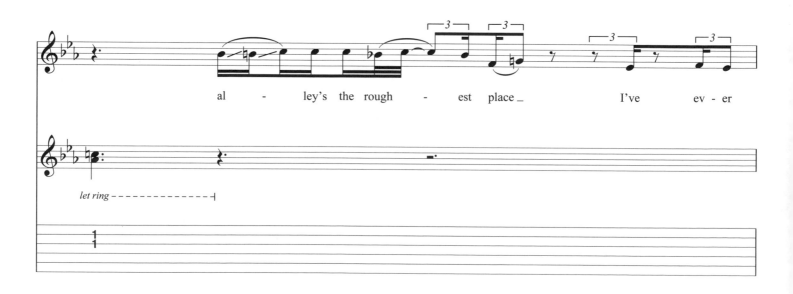

al - ley's the rough - est place ___ I've ev - er

let ring - - - - - - - - - -

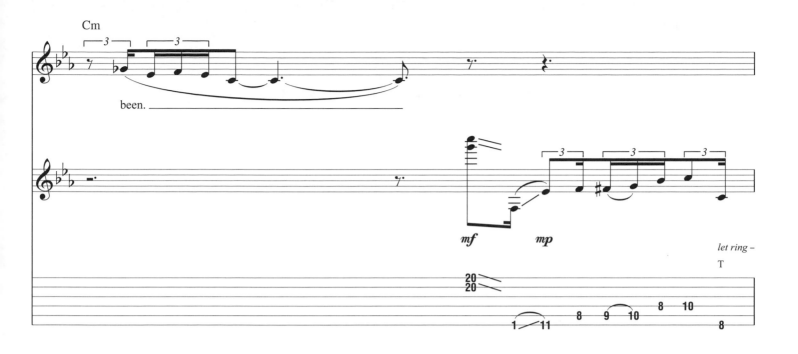

been.

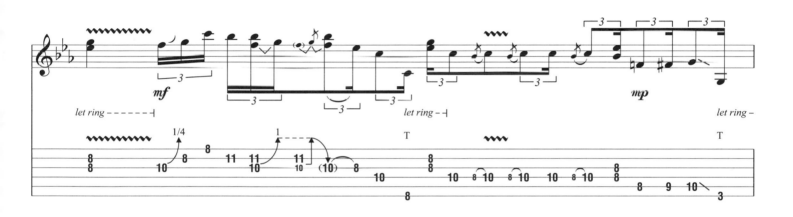

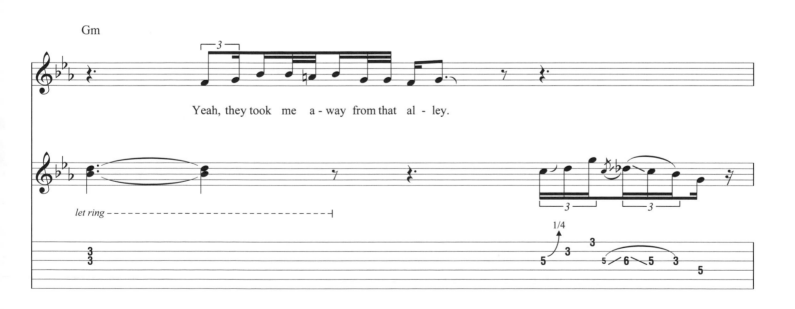

Yeah, they took me a - way from that al - ley.

Lord,_ they took me right back _____ to the bend._

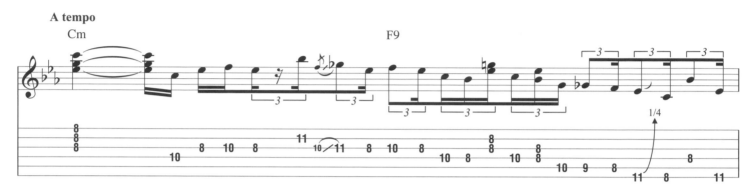

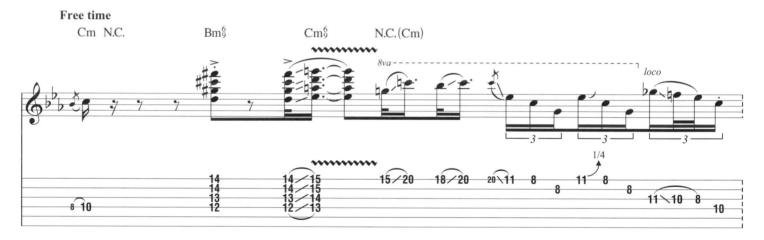

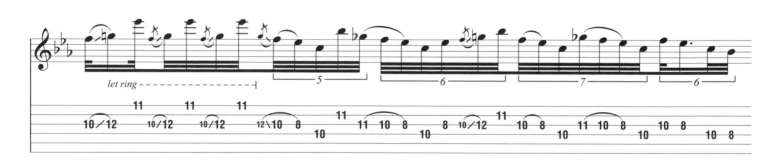

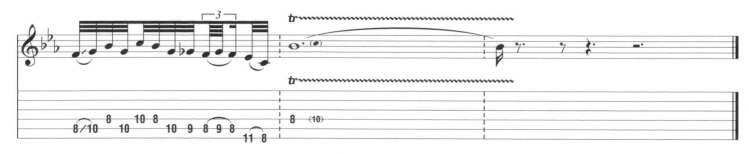

94

GUITAR NOTATION LEGEND

THE MUSICAL STAFF shows pitches and rhythms and is divided by bar lines into measures. Pitches are named after the first seven letters of the alphabet.

TABLATURE graphically represents the guitar fingerboard. Each horizontal line represents a string, and each number represents a fret.

4th string, 2nd fret   1st & 2nd strings open, played together   open D chord

HALF-STEP BEND: Strike the note and bend up 1/2 step.

WHOLE-STEP BEND: Strike the note and bend up one step.

GRACE NOTE BEND: Strike the note and immediately bend up as indicated.

SLIGHT (MICROTONE) BEND: Strike the note and bend up 1/4 step.

BEND AND RELEASE: Strike the note and bend up as indicated, then release back to the original note. Only the first note is struck.

PRE-BEND: Bend the note as indicated, then strike it.

VIBRATO: The string is vibrated by rapidly bending and releasing the note with the fretting hand.

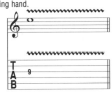

PALM MUTING: The note is partially muted by the pick hand lightly touching the string(s) just before the bridge.

HAMMER-ON: Strike the first (lower) note with one finger, then sound the higher note (on the same string) with another finger by fretting it without picking.

PULL-OFF: Place both fingers on the notes to be sounded. Strike the first note and without picking, pull the finger off to sound the second (lower) note.

LEGATO SLIDE: Strike the first note and then slide the same fret-hand finger up or down to the second note. The second note is not struck.

SHIFT SLIDE: Same as legato slide, except the second note is struck.

TRILL: Very rapidly alternate between the notes indicated by continuously hammering on and pulling off.

TAPPING: Hammer ("tap") the fret indicated with the pick-hand index or middle finger and pull off to the note fretted by the fret hand.

NATURAL HARMONIC: Strike the note while the fret-hand lightly touches the string directly over the fret indicated.

PINCH HARMONIC: The note is fretted normally and a harmonic is produced by adding the edge of the thumb or the tip of the index finger of the pick hand to the normal pick attack.

TREMOLO PICKING: The note is picked as rapidly and continuously as possible.

VIBRATO BAR DIVE AND RETURN: The pitch of the note or chord is dropped a specified number of steps (in rhythm), then returned to the original pitch.

VIBRATO BAR SCOOP: Depress the bar just before striking the note, then quickly release the bar.

VIBRATO BAR DIP: Strike the note and then immediately drop a specified number of steps, then release back to the original pitch.

Additional Musical Definitions

(accent) • Accentuate note (play it louder).

 (staccato) • Play the note short.

D.S. al Coda • Go back to the sign (𝄋), then play until the measure marked "***To Coda***," then skip to the section labelled "**Coda**."

D.C. al Fine • Go back to the beginning of the song and play until the measure marked "***Fine***" (end).

Fill • Label used to identify a brief melodic figure which is to be inserted into the arrangement.

N.C. • Harmony is implied.

 • Repeat measures between signs.

 • When a repeated section has different endings, play the first ending only the first time and the second ending only the second time.